Leading Without Leading

By Wayne Goldsmith

Leading Without Leading

At last a book which shows you how to lead by not doing it

By Wayne Goldsmith

wayne@moregold.com.au

Published: 2018

Publisher: WG Coaching

ISBN: 9781980980759

Table of Contents

Acknowledgement

This book is dedicated to all the leaders I've known—the good and the bad, the inspirational and the destructive, the innovative and the conservative, the visionary and the limited. I've learnt something from all of you.

Some of the best leaders I've known didn't even know they were leaders or leading at the time. And I've known some terrible leaders. Leaders who don't deserve to be called leaders any more than someone who re-heats left-over take-away food deserves to be known as a gourmet chef.

Leadership comes in many shapes and forms. When I talk leadership with high school students, the session usually begins with a group brainstorm about what leadership is, how to recognise a leader, what a leader does, and examples of people the students believe are great leaders.

During one of these sessions, I asked a group of boys to provide examples of great leaders—people they'd read about, seen on TV, studied at school, or people they knew and thought showed good leadership qualities.

One boy stood up and said with pride and emotion that his mother was the best leader he knew. I asked him why he felt his mum was such a good leader. He answered that it was because there were seven kids in his family. "Our dad left us when I was three years old and all of us were under 12," he said. "My mum has raised us with no help, working three jobs and she never complains, never whines. She just works as hard as she can to give us everything we could ever need," he said and sat down, wiping away a tear.

I realised at that moment the way we've looked at leadership is all wrong. Here's a single mother, facing immense pressures, challenges, emotions and the day-to-day grind of paying bills, working three jobs, raising seven young children and her son stands up in front of his peers—a room full of teenage boys—and says my mother is the best leader he knows.

Not only is his mum remarkable in more ways than many of us could imagine–but *her* leadership–has inspired *his leadership*. He may well now become an outstanding leader in his own right because of the leadership qualities he sees his mother display day in and day out.

His mother had never done a leadership training program. She'd never read a book by some leadership guru. She'd never been through a series of leadership workshops, webinars, seminars or any other kinds of '-ars'. But, she's as great a leader as anyone could hope to meet in their lives.

Her commitment, her dedication, her integrity, her work ethic, her compassion, her love, her relentless and tireless drive to provide a decent life for her family is the essence of leadership, but she'll never hold political office, become a CEO of a listed company or coach a professional sports team to win an Olympic gold medal.

And there are people like her everywhere. Anyone can lead… they just don't know it. Anyone.

People don't know they can lead because leadership has been sold as something only famous or rich or successful or talented people can do: as something you need to learn, to do a course about, to study, or to purchase as a program.

Leadership is found anywhere–everywhere: you just need to look for it.

Sometimes leadership hides in the most humble of people and in the most unsuspecting places you could imagine. I worked in a factory that made car radiators. The 'boss' was the only guy in the place who wore a tie and that made him important. He sat in his office, did secret boss stuff and the last thing you wanted was to be called in there. As a 17-year-old, the boss terrified me. I got anxious when he walked past and said good morning.

I assumed he was a good leader because he *was* the leader. I didn't know what a leader did or was supposed to do, but this guy was one because he was one.

To this day I have no idea who the guy was, what his leadership philosophies were, what he felt about the industry, how he got where he was, or how he chose his tie each morning, but he was my first boss.

But he wasn't my first 'leader'. In the same factory was an old guy called Fred or 'Old Fred' or 'Freddy', depending on how well you knew him. He was the cleaner, the guy who seemed to know where everything was, the guy who filled in where ever he was needed. He was *the* guy. He seemed to be part of the place. Everyone knew him. He was quiet and seemed a little shy, but everyone seemed to like him.

One Saturday, I stayed back and do a little extra work. It was just me and Fred. He had a little office down the back of the storeroom and he invited me in for a cup of tea before we started work.

On the wall was a photo. It was—or at least it seemed to be—a picture of Fred... but he was wearing the robes and wig of a barrister. I made a crack; "Hey Fred, nice costume!" It was an attempt to be funny, the sort of reaction you'd expect from a smart-ass 17-year-old in his first job with no idea about the world.

Fred smiled and replied; "That's me. I used to be a lawyer."

After another two or three wisecracks, I asked him to tell me his story.

He said; "I was a lawyer for 30 years. Made a lot of money. Travelled a lot. Lived in a huge house in one of the best suburbs in the city. Had everything any man could ever want or need."

Incredulous, I had to ask the most obvious question, the only question you could ask; "so why are you working here?! You're a lawyer. You could do anything. Why here? They make you clean up stuff and do all the crappy jobs no one else wants to do. Why would you work here?"

"Because here I can be Fred," he replied. "I just turn up. I do what needs to be done at my own pace. I talk to lots of people, people who don't expect anything from me, people who just want to talk about their work, their kids, their cars, their hobbies, the news, their sports team... and I love that. And when I walk out of here at night, I don't take anything with me. I don't have to worry about being someone I don't want to be or doing stuff I don't like doing. This is the best job I've ever had."

I was still stunned.

He continued; "I'm going to tell you something. It's up to you what you think about it. But I've watched you for a while now. You're a smart guy. You've got a lot going for you. But everyone in this place knows you don't want to be here. You hate this place. Every time I stop and talk with you it's always about how much you hate the job, how terrible the work is, how you wish you could do something else. But until you stop complaining about this place and start following your own path, you'll never go anywhere... and you and me will still be here doing this in 20 years."

No one had ever spoken to me with such honesty—except for my dad—and well... no one ever listens to their dad.

I said; "Fred. I failed high school. I failed it about as much as anyone can fail it. This is the only job I can get."

And then came the bullet right between the eyes. "You've got a choice. The only thing behind you is your ass. Your ass is for sitting on, and for not much else. If you look backwards, you'll always just be the guy who failed high school," said Fred.

"I knew some impressive people when I was a lawyer. I met the prime minister. Even met the Queen. Rich people. Important people. Famous people. You know the one thing they all had in common? They looked forward. All of them. Whenever I spoke to them it was always about what they would do, what they were dreaming of, about things they wanted to achieve, about the places they were going... all of them thought about, talked about and walked towards their dreams. You... you whine and complain and sulk about how awful this place is and how you wish life was different. Well, it can be, but it's up to you."

I felt like I'd been hit in the guts with a giant marshmallow. It was both confronting, challenging and somehow–it felt right.

"Fred," I ventured, "can you help me?"

"Sure," he said. "From now on, whenever you and I talk, I only want to hear about your dreams. I am not interested in talking with you about this place or how much you hate it here or any other such rubbish. When you say, 'Morning Fred', the next words out of your mouth need to be something to do with where you're going or something you're dreaming about or something you're learning, or if not, you'll find out that your ass is good for one thing other than sitting on, a kick from my boot!"

I remember thinking about that conversation over and over, and now, almost 40 years later, I still think about it.

I remember when I next saw Fred. I said; "Morning Fred. I've decided I'm going study and get a better job. One in the city that pays a lot more money."

He smiled deeply and said; "That's great news. Where are you going to study? When does the course start? Have you enrolled yet? That's such great news Wayne. Good on you."

And that was it. Everything had changed. A short conversation with an old guy—the guy who cleaned up everyone else's mess, the guy who just seemed to potter around the factory doing all those dirty, boring, dull jobs no one wanted to do—changed my life.

And I learnt something else. I talked to a few other people around the place about Fred. And he'd had the same talk with them. You know 'the' talk. The one about how you could be anything, do anything, go anywhere, be anyone, achieve everything if only you are prepared to believe in yourself and work hard.

The guy with the tie was the boss, but Fred was the leader. He was the guy who inspired you to be all you could be by connecting with you as an individual. Fred was the one person you could talk to who understood that leadership isn't about doing leadership courses or having the corner office and it's certainly not about wearing a tie: it's being yourself, discovering your own dreams, believing that dreams can come true and leading yourself—and others—towards those dreams.

Leadership is subtle. Leadership is quiet. Leadership is personal. Leadership is natural. Once you realise that, most of what we've thought about, talked about and done in the area of leadership training is wrong. Leadership is simply the ability to inspire change in yourself and others, and, in so doing, turn everything around.

So, Fred—this book is for you. Thank you.

Chapter One

The Lead in

It is estimated that there were about ten million books written and published in the world last year. It is also estimated, that of those ten million books, around 9,999,000 were on leadership. The rest were cooking books, self-help books and sporting biographies. And just check out some of these titles:

How to lead, when to lead, who to lead, why to lead—all your leadership questions answered.

The 45,690 qualities of great leaders.

The ten-top tips for being a tip-top leader.

Learn to lead a listed company in three minutes or double your money back.

You can't spell leader without 'e'.

How wombats lead.

Leadership — the new black.

Quantum physics and the new leadership: what electrons know about leadership.

You can't lead Generation X, Y and I without starting with the ABC and some DIY.

Great military leadership models and how driving a tank through the office makes you the boss.

LEAD: Lead by Eating Apples and Dieting.

And so many more…

It seems like everyone is writing a book about leading, leaders, leadership, taking the lead, being a leader, teaching leaders, coaching leaders, growing leaders, leading from the front, leading from the back, leading from the side, leading from below, leading leaders, learning lessons from leaders and leading from the lead. The funny thing is; leadership, as we know it, no longer exists. We are killing off millions of trees, destroying the rainforests and increasing global warming to produce the paper to write about leadership but we are writing about something that is no longer relevant. Leadership has changed and has changed at such an alarming rate it probably needs a new name. Seeing as no one has been smart enough to come up with one yet, let's give *Leading Without Leading* a go.

Leading Without Leading—lessons from great comedians

There is a great *Seinfeld* episode where Jerry and George are sitting in a diner talking about the possibility of writing a TV show for NBC. In the discussion, they are kicking ideas back and forward, brainstorming potential themes for the show. George says; "Let's do a show about nothing." At first Jerry looks at him like he has gone crazy, then thinks about it and says; "I think you may have something."

This book is about nothing, too!

Well, it's about nothing if you want to learn how to lead the old way. If you want inspiration on how to lead, or get a blueprint on leading, or read stories by the leaders of the world's biggest companies, or learn a lot of catchy sayings like 'learning to lead is leading to learn', then there is nothing in this book for you.

If you are reading this introduction while standing in an airport bookstore trying to decide whether to buy it, put it back on the shelf where you found it and move on to the *789 Most Popular Leadership Quotes* book, a few metres to your left and only $29.95 (make sure you get a tax invoice).

However; if you are interested in where leadership is going, if you are passionate about making a real difference to the people you work with and the organisation you work for, if you are someone who embraces change and enhancing performance through learning and innovation, if you are someone who accepts there are no limits to excellence and no boundaries to what is possible, then you are in the right place.

In the Monty Python film, *Life of Brian*, Brian is hailed as the new Messiah. In one scene, a large crowd gathers outside his home to hear his wisdom and listen to his teachings about life, the universe and other stuff. When he emerges at the window, the crowed hushes and he speaks. "You don't need to follow me. You don't need to follow anybody. You are all different. You are all individuals. You've got to work it out for yourselves."

That's what this book is about. Leadership is not leading. It's being yourself. Leading is not about following a model or a script or a clever training course or learning ten lessons in effective leadership. It's about you.

The greatest assets to any organisation are thinking, creative, innovative individuals who are passionate about learning and growing and developing as human beings. If they work together as a team—that's great. If they can recite the company mission statement, values, virtues and sing the company theme song in perfect harmony—fantastic. But how terrific would it be to have every person, every individual, every unique human being, working to their full potential, enjoying what they do and unleashing their own brand of genius to enhance your organisation's performance?

In this book, we will smash a lot of the old stuff–all the old stuff we believed were modern leadership 'must haves':

Mission statements… gone.

Corporate values lists… exploded.

Motivation lectures… extinct.

Leadership modelling… dead and buried.

Systems-based organisations… you have to go.

Team building… crashed and burnt.

Culture development… ka-boom.

Change management processes… shot through the heart.

We will challenge the billions of words and millions of pages in the 9,999,000 leadership books published last year and come up with some simple but effective alternatives in just one book.

While it is tempting to overkill the *Leading Without Leading* theme by leaving the rest of this book blank, here are 100-plus pages of words and pictures to keep you interested and make you feel the money you spent was worth it—it was.

Story time...

I was working with a professional football team. One of the best players—one of the talented star athletes in the team—was an Indigenous Australian player. While he could do remarkable things with the ball, he was very quiet, hated speaking publicly, shunned the media, and was content to just play football.

Speaking with him one-on-one was easy! He was a deep-thinking, intelligent guy with a great sense of humour and he was immensely popular in the team. But he struggled to speak to large groups, so, a result, he was always overlooked for leadership roles.

During pre-season training the team was discussing which players to include in the leadership group for the coming season. I suggested the Indigenous player would make an excellent leader. The head coach thought about this for a while and said the player could only be included in the leadership team if he underwent extensive leadership training, including a lot of education in the areas of public speaking, media management and group leadership techniques.

I challenged the head coach; "What's the purpose of leadership?"

He replied; "To lead"

I responded; "Exactly. But what does 'to lead' actually look like?"

The head coach said; "We know players are leading well when they influence other players to do the right things, to do them the right way and at the right time."

"And how," I asked, "do players influence other players?"

"By spending time with them, by working with them, by building relationships with them, by mentoring them and by leading by example," said the head coach.

"So," I suggested. "If what we really need from this player is his ability to influence other players, why does he need to do a public speaking course? What he really needs is the opportunity to subtly–quietly influence other players in a way he's comfortable with, where his natural ability to connect with other people can flourish and where he can lead his way."

And so, we appointed him to the leadership team.

When the need to influence the behaviours and attitudes of team members arose, instead of standing up and spruiking the same old messages about hard-work and commitment to a room full of his team mates in the way more traditional leaders might have done, he would invite players–one at a time–to kick the ball with him at the end of practice—just him and one other player—and while they were kicking, they'd just talk quietly, intently and purposefully.

The Indigenous player became the most influential and the most effective leader in the team without ever doing a leadership training program.

LESSONS IN NOT LEADING—WHAT DIDN'T YOU LEARN?

1. Leadership is the art of subtle influence.
2. Leadership is the art of inspiring change through honest, authentic, emotional connection.
3. Everyone can lead—in their own way. You've just got to let them.

Chapter Two

Why do what we do when we don't know why we are doing it?

Pick a company. Any company. OK, don't tell which one. I will guess. Just answer a few questions:

Does your company have a leadership training program?

Does your company run team building exercises, team breakout sessions, team retreats and team development workshops?

Does your company run induction workshops and orientation days where everyone learns the company mission statement, values and virtues, policies and procedures, rules and regulations?

Does your company have slogans, sayings, motivational signs and similar posters around the office, factory, lunchroom, etc?

Does your company rely on systems and rules and structures which must be precisely implemented?

Does your company run innovation and creativity enhancement break-outs?

Does your company hold annual change management workshops?

Does your company offer professional development courses and programs?

Let me guess…

Your company isn't progressing, isn't improving, isn't growing.

Your company has a problem recruiting and retaining staff.

It performs nowhere near where it could.

People spend a lot of time moaning about what's wrong with the place.

People don't work to their full potential.

People are reluctant to attend training programs, workshops and learning activities and, when they do they learn next to nothing.

People who attend your training sessions and breakout weekends come back saying; "Well, that was a waste of time."

People drag down and 'tall poppy' the legs of the leaders instead of rallying behind them and helping them be the best leaders they can.

Ka-ching! I win. The name of your company is… (insert the name of practically any organisation in the world here). How can that be?

You are doing everything you are supposed to be doing. You are following the golden rules of human resources, staff training and development. Why isn't it working?

You have ticked all the professional training and development boxes, but nothing is changing. What are you doing wrong?

You have bought all books, watched all the training videos and attended all the NLP, VIP, RSVP, POQ, DOA and RIP courses money could buy. What is happening?

Relax. You're among friends. You could play the same game in just about any organisation, any political party, any sporting team, any school, any club, any company, anywhere in the world and come up with the same answers.

Why? Because we do what we think we are supposed to do—what everyone else says we are supposed to do—not what we really need to do. We spend a lot of time ticking boxes, organising workshops, creating clinics, convening conferences, developing learning experiences and implementing programs because we are afraid not to.

Why are we doing a staff leadership training program? Because that's what everyone else does. Why are we getting in a motivational speaker? Because that's what everyone else does. Why are we having a day off site to come up with a corporate mission statement? Because that's what everyone else does. (Surely, you can't run a great business without a great mission statement on the website!)

In fact, some of the world's most innovative and creative organisations get that way by doing what everyone else does but just more often than anyone else can, i.e. they're not that innovative and creative, they've just got enough money to do a lot more of the old stuff.

What a waste. What a terrible waste of time. Time, money, effort, energy and time (I said time twice because in reality it is the most precious thing you have to waste). The reason the 'we-do-it-because-everyone-else-does-it' stuff does not make a real difference is because it's everyone else's stuff!

It's like benchmarking; waste of time, waste of energy, waste of money, waste of effort. Why? Because it someone else's 'bench'. Just remember that the only thing that leaves 'bench marks' are people's butts. The butts of the people sitting still on those benches. Benchmarking has become trendy—CEOs, managers and board members heading off on jolly junkets to other companies, other organisations and other countries to learn what they do that makes them so successful. They are all hunting the same thing; miracle changes, instant innovations, quick-fix ideas and guaranteed-to-succeed systems which will create success at home. And, without exception, they are wasting their time, money and energy.

First, if you were heading a successful organisation, why would you share your secrets with a potential competitor? You might tell them what you did in the past, but not what you plan to do. Think about it for a moment. If you had an innovative idea or revolutionary new product line, would you give it away to another organisation for a couple of cappuccinos and a sandwich over lunch?

Second, as it is usually administrators and management who do these benchmarking junkets, they generally lack the technical knowledge and industry-specific understanding to make significant, meaningful, relevant changes to the performance systems of their own organisations.

Third, and most important, you cannot copy a successful system from another organisation and make it work in yours. Again, you cannot copy a successful system from another organisation and make it work in yours. And one more time, you cannot copy a successful system from another organisation and make it work in yours.

But everyone tries. Everyone thinks there's a one-size-fits-all, guaranteed-to-work, never-fail solution to their problems in another place, another city or in another country. People try to buy success by copying from other people who they feel are successful.

Copying kills! The single most important quality in greatness is uniqueness. It's about thinking differently and thinking different things. Copying kills.

A great sports coach I worked with said; "There are three types of athletes at the Olympic games. There are those who are not competitive, who do not understand what it takes to win and never will. Then there are those who go to the Games and lose, but then try to copy the winners. These athletes are doomed to fail because they are copying what's working now so will always be four years behind the gold medallists. And there are the winners. Those who four years ago had the vision to see what it would take to win, made it happen and reaped the rewards of leading the sport to new levels of performance."

So, what's the message? Do it your own way. You have to. Do it your own way.

Every time you use a photocopier, the words and pictures become less clear and harder to see than on the original. It's the same with ideas. Every time they get copied, their original meaning and clarity and relevance fades.

So, what's the alternative? Stop copying. You need not copy anyone or anything. Tap into the expertise, passion, drive, enthusiasm, knowledge and skills that exist in every organisation. Release the genius that lives in every person in your organisation. Do it your own way.

Organisations are not buildings. They are not training rooms. They are not quality assurance systems, KPIs or management training programs. They are not workshops—the only workshops that make sense are those involved in light engineering. Organisations are people. People with unique needs. People with unique attitudes. People with unique identities. People with unique motivations. People from different cultures, some with different languages and faiths.

The three most important things you need to make your organisation successful are all the same–people, people, people.

The reason training programs and courses and workshops and breakouts and lectures do not work is that they do not provide avenues for the uniqueness of your people to be expressed or engaged, let alone enhanced, exhilarated and exalted.

The key to creating a more effective organisation is to encourage, embrace and unleash the unlimited power and genius inside everyone who works there.

This is the new leadership:

Where leaders once lectured, they now listen.

Where leaders once enforced, they now engage and empower.

Where leaders once trained others, they now grow with them.

Where leaders once politicised, they now partner.

Where leaders once disciplined, they now discover what people need.

Where leaders once took responsibility, they now share it.

Where leaders once indoctrinated, they now innovate.

Where leaders once implemented rigid systems, they now create opportunities to enhance them.

Where leaders once created, they now provide the environment and opportunity for their people to be creative.

Everyone can and will lead in their own way and utilise the talent and gifts they possess when given the right opportunity and environment and a lot of trust, faith and belief.

The sales rep talking with clients is leading the organisation as she talks about products and services. The receptionist talking to people who call or walk in the front door is leading the organisation as he meets and greets them. The old guy opening and closing the security gates at the entrance to the company car park is leading the organisation as he welcomes guests and directs them to a space. They are leading the organisation–in the same sense that the general manager decides about company programs, the chairman of the board leads a discussion on company strategies and the head accountant decides how to best manage the company budget. Everyone leads in their own way and in a way which releases their full potential.

Once you stop looking at leadership as a role for senior management and something only a few gifted people can possess, once you stop believing this 'leaders are born' rubbish, once you make a real commitment to unleash the potential in *everyone* in the organisation, then you will be unstoppable.

Story time...

I was asked to work with a professional football team who felt they'd nailed the mission statement, vision and values thing. They'd enlisted the services of a world renowned and respected management consulting firm, worked through the mission statement workshop exercises and organisational values breakout sessions, and, as a result, all over the building, the change rooms, the gymnasium, on their stationery, business cards—everywhere you looked—the new mission statement and corporate values were displayed.

Their three corporate values were communication, respect and professionalism.

On my first visit to the team, I walked up to the reception desk. The receptionist was talking on the phone. It was clear the other caller was a friend. The receptionist smiled at me and waved for me to wait. I waited. And waited. And waited… for six minutes while the receptionist continued the personal phone call. In the time I was waiting, I could hear other lines ringing—possibly new or existing customers or fans or sponsors or the media. The calls all went unanswered.

When the receptionist finished the personal call, they asked, "Excuse me, who are you? Who are you meeting?"

I let her know my name was Wayne, and that I was there to meet Mrs Johnson in the football department.

The receptionist replied; "Who?"

I repeated my previous reply.

The receptionist responded; "Take a seat".

After another five minutes, the receptionist called through to Mrs Johnson and announced my arrival.

While I sat, I watched people coming and going. No one said hello to me or to anyone else. No one dressed in the team colours or in team clothing.

A player walked past me and tried to get in the door into the head office and found it locked. He turned to the receptionist and said; "Open the f#%*@n door will ya!"

After he left, the receptionist called someone, apparently another member of staff and spent the next few minutes saying less than complimentary words about the player who had been locked out.

Twenty minutes later, Mrs Johnson emerged, welcomed me and invited me to follow her to her office.

When I got to my appointment, I asked Mrs Johnson—the architect of the new mission statement, corporate values process—how the new corporate culture development program was going?

She replied, "Great. We've got a fantastic team of people who are all committed to our sustainable success as an organisation. Everyone has embraced our new corporate values."

I said; "Your values have no value."

A little shocked she asked; "How can you say that? We've got a great set of values."

"Values have no value unless they are lived by everyone in the organisation. Values only have value when visitors or fans or sponsors or media walk in the front door and can see and feel the values through the words and actions of everyone in your team," I responded: "People will only believe in values if they are 'their' values. Once individuals take ownership of values and understand the behaviours and actions that show those values in everything they do, things change. Shiny new signs and new corporate brochures announcing a shift to a values-based corporate culture make no difference. It comes down to how each individual believes in those values and how those values effect their attitudes and behaviours."

LESSONS IN NOT LEADING—WHAT DIDN'T YOU LEARN?

1. Do it your own way.

2. Tap into the potential of your people.

3. Everyone can lead in their own way.

Chapter Three

The how and why of leading without leading: how leadership has changed

In the past, knowledge about leadership was limited to just a few. You learnt about it in the military, or in management school, or at university, or in training programs for company executives. Our models and understanding of what a leader is were largely based on the traditional Julius Caesar-, General Patton-, Winston Churchill-, CEO-, Presidential-type leader. They spoke, people did what they said, and all was well in leadership land.

Let's have another look at the leadership wisdom of *Seinfeld*.

George and Jerry are still talking about their show about nothing. Jerry says; "The show can't be about nothing—it has to be about something."

George says; "Ok, what did you today?"

Jerry replies; "Well I got up, I made breakfast, I did some shopping, then I came here."

"That's a show," says George.

That's leadership.

The new leadership is not an act or a speech or a lecture or a board report. It's not a title or an award or a qualification. It's not a program, procedures, a policy or a product. It's you and what you do every day. It's who you are and the way you live your life. It's the standards you set for your own life and how you maintain those standards over the 100 years or so of your existence.

The new leadership is not conforming to a leadership style or system or program. It's not going to a course and learning how to be like some other leader, it's about embracing your uniqueness, unleashing your own potential and being who you are.

Why is this so? you may ask. A quick look at the papers, the television and a few books will tell you: the old leadership model just does not work. The old model, the one-size-fits-all, lead from the front model, is based on a few people having a large amount of information. Today things are very different. Today we have a large number of people with an incredible amount of information. Today anyone can get anything, anytime, anywhere and usually for free and right in the palm of their hand on their phone, their tablet, their laptop: anything, anywhere, anytime.

Knowledge is no longer power because everyone has knowledge. The real power now is in the five Cs:

· Creativity: thinking things, saying things and doing things no one else is thinking, saying or doing.

· Connection: connecting with people and understanding their needs—being customer focused and client orientated.

· Communication: communicating often—and communicating with people when, where and how they want to be communicated with.

· Collaboration: being able to build effective thinking, learning and problem-solving teams.

· Change: being able to accelerate your rate of learning and change faster than your opponents.

Of all the Cs, change is the most important for leadership.

Human beings are wired to do three things: to think, to communicate and to act.

Thinking, that's the easy part. Lots of people live in their heads, but thinking about doing something new or different or worthwhile is as far as it goes. They wish things would change. They hope things might change. They dream about things changing, but mostly their desire for change remains nothing more than wishes, hopes and dreams.

And talking, that's pretty simple too. The world is full of people who talk a great talk. Open Google and click your way through to YouTube. There are millions of people keen to talk to you about all manner of things.

But, it's the doing that matters. It's action that changes the world. It's taking the big step from the mind and mouth to movement that has produced all the brilliant and amazing things our species has produced.

You need to understand change and how universal access to knowledge and information has changed leadership, and the world (for the better), forever. Before the printing press, access to the latest knowledge and information was limited to a privileged few in the church and aristocracy. Until then, most people believed what they were told and lacked the knowledge and information to challenge the status quo.

Then along comes Gutenberg, who whacks together the first printing press is his shed in his spare time, and knowledge and information becomes available to more people—people with different backgrounds, attitudes and beliefs. These people start to read, analyse and think for themselves. The potential of people becomes a powerful tool for social change.

Skip ahead a few hundred years and along comes the Internet. Millions around the world can now read about everything and anything, anytime, anywhere. Knowledge and information moves at an incredible rate all over the world. Everyone knows what you know. There are no secrets, no surprises, no shocks.

In the past, knowledge was power—information was everything. Now, knowledge changes so quickly, and access to information is so easy, that knowledge is no longer the source of power it once was.

In the past, people—particularly rich people, powerful people, politicians, the clergy, and academics—hoarded knowledge and used it to progress their own agenda. They learnt as much as they could and then hid it away, releasing it little by little for their own political or financial advantage.

Life has changed. Knowledge moves faster than a chocolate moves from my seven-year-old's hand to his mouth. Some genius comes up with an idea to change the world at 6am in Scotland and kids in Botswana are talking about it ten minutes later. A rugby coach in South Africa develops the world's most brilliant try scoring move on Monday morning and by Wednesday afternoon players in Fiji have not only learnt it but improved on it and plan to use against the South Africans next time the two teams meet. You wake up in Auckland, read the London Times online, find a great article on education, email a link to the article to a teacher friend in New York who prints it out and reads it to his class of eight year olds, and they already have a copy and are writing a rebuttal piece back to the London Times.

In this environment, the *what* of life (knowledge) is no longer the key to success. In the past, the *what* you did—your knowledge, qualifications, degrees, certificates and awards—were the difference between you and the rest of the market. The more *what* you knew the better chance you had of being successful.

Now it is all about *how* you do *what* you do. And of course, *how* is leadership. *How* relates to passion, commitment, perseverance, attitude, integrity, communication, enjoyment, consistency, honesty, quality—people things. Performance is about people not points, percentages, promotions or profits.

In this environment, leadership now belongs to everyone. People now own the concept of leadership and now, more than ever, people want their leaders to change. People want leaders who can change as fast, or faster than they can.

So, *how* are we going to change the world of leadership?

Story time...

I was working with a football team that lived, trained and played in a hot, humid climate. One of the big issues for the team was hydration—drinking enough fluid to stay healthy and train and play to the best of their ability in their home environment.

We invited a world-respected sports nutritionist to talk with the team. The nutritionist was highly-regarded, well-credentialed and experienced. We brought the team together and the doctor spoke about the importance of hydration, how much to drink, when to drink, the issues around drinking alcohol for athletes, and the sugar content of drinks. It was an outstanding presentation with brilliant power point slides and the latest research findings on this important topic. Yet, none of the players changed their hydration habits.

So, we invited another expert. She was considered the leading sports nutritionist in the field and, once again, the team came together and listened to a professional and well-delivered presentation about hydration. And again, none of the players changed their behaviour. It was time to try something different.

The players who were the worst in terms of their hydration behaviour were the younger players—the rookies and second year professionals. Unlike the more senior players, they hadn't learnt the importance of taking care of their bodies.

We invited a few of the more senior players together and asked them to do one thing. Every time they took a drink at training, or when they were travelling, or when they were around their younger team mates, to get them a drink too. Our intent was to subtly and quietly influence the hydration behaviour of the youngsters.

Within a week everyone's behaviour had changed. The team was performing better in the hot humid conditions and had a very successful year.

This is the real power of leadership: the power of people to change people. Not through talking. Not by buying them books and biographies about leadership. But through the art of subtly influencing the behaviours of others—and by being the change you want to see.

LESSONS IN NOT LEADING—WHAT DIDN'T YOU LEARN?

1. Lead yourself.

2. Success is a moving target.

3. How you do it is more important than what you do.

Chapter Four

Ninety-nine percent of our problems are due to old leadership models; the other one percent is global warming

The world right now, it seems, is talking itself into a one crisis after another. And it is the leaders who are doing the most talking.

Political leaders, corporate leaders, business leaders, social leaders and religious leaders are all talking doom and gloom and preparing people for the worst.

When leaders should provide the environment and the opportunity for individuals to believe in themselves and to think and act positively to change the world with courage, innovation and determination, leaders are thinking, saying and doing the opposite.

Write a list of the people who have stood up in the last few months and said; "The world is full of opportunity. You as an individual can do anything. Keep dreaming. Believe in yourself. Change the things you can change. Now is the greatest time of your life."

Short list, isn't it? Just three on mine—LeBron James, Oprah and the bloke who lives a few houses down who just won second prize in the lottery. And this is why our tired, outdated and sick leadership models and practices have to go. Because we have relied on leaders to tell us what to do and when, where, how and why to do it, we have forgotten—or maybe never learnt, to lead ourselves.

Without reading ahead, write the top-five problems facing the corporate world right now. Here is a little writing Muzak to help pass the time while you write your list: "Tall and tan and young and lovely, the girl from Ipanema goes walking......." OK, finished?

Did your list contain any or all of the following?

1. A lack of innovative leaders with vision who have a future focus
2. Succession planning
3. An inability to communicate across successive generations
4. A lack of responsibility
5. Finding and keeping great people—Gain, Train and Retain

These issues are all due to our loyalty to the old leadership models and our resistance to changing the way we look at leadership. Let's look at them.

1. A lack of innovative leaders with real vision—who have a real future focus.

If leadership is about one thing, it's the future. Take a look at the word; leader. We all know what it means, we all learnt it when we were five years old. When you were a kid, you played follow the leader. Who was the leader? The kid who went first, the innovator, the kid who changed the direction and speed and way of doing things.

When did we enjoy the game? When the person who went first changed things, when they did something we weren't expecting, when they challenged us to do things differently—to go in different directions and in different ways and at different speeds than we had gone before.

So, what do leaders do? They—ta-dah—LEAD.

Now we spend so much time, effort and energy training leaders to lead like all the other leaders that no one is focusing on the future of leadership.

Instead of encouraging our leaders to lead us in new directions and to enjoy the changes they are bringing in, we try to make them go in the same direction as everyone else. It's like playing follow the leader down a tube; "we are happy for you to lead and we will follow you as long as you keep going in this direction."

Leaders of organisations will tell you they are futurists, but in reality, they are "things are going great the way things are—how I set them up—and instead of changing things and being more innovative than the opposition, we will just tinker, fiddle and adjust them slightly – ists".

Leaders are visionaries. Why do they call a vision a vision? Because you can see it! Leaders see the future—they see it with such clarity and such detail that to them it's as if it's already happened.

This is the real difference between leadership and management. Leadership is about the future, about seeing the future, seeing it first, and leading yourself and others towards that future. Management is about creating the environment and building the opportunity for the things that need to happen to create that fabulous future to happen.

Why do visionary leaders surround themselves with outstanding managers? Because outstanding managers have the skills, knowledge and experience to act now, they live in the present, and in doing so, ensure the vision becomes a reality.

Leadership is about *tomorrow*: Management is about *today*.

There's a brilliant quote from De Bono; "At each stage in civilisation the guardians of the culture are convinced that the best of all states has been achieved and that further progress will be limited to minor adjustments. Because of this thinking, the thinking becomes realistic—as a self-fulfilling prophecy."

Despite overwhelming evidence that the most successful people, organisations and companies need to continue to speed up their rate of change throughout their existence or face failure and collapse, most leaders just tinker, adjust and play with minor changes believing they have all the answers.

Most leaders don't understand the fundamental concept of real change—that is—that you actually have to change! And the more successful you want your organisation to be, the more frequent and more radical the change must be.

All of us have, at one time, thought, "This place needs to change," or, "If this place changed the way we do XYZ we could succeed," or, "If I was the boss, man I would change this and that and this place could be brilliant," or, "This guy (the CEO) has no idea. If I ran this company, things would be different."

Then you become a CEO or managing director and what happens? You become the person you always said you wouldn't! You become the leader you spent the past 20 years rubbishing. You become the person you used to spend time warning others about.

2. Succession planning.

This is a huge problem for organisations all over the world. And why? We all think it's because there are no great new leaders coming through the system.

We believe Generation Y or Generation I (as in Internet, I-phone, I-pad and what I want) is disorganised, disgruntled, disturbed, dis-engaged and disruptive or that the management training systems are all missing the point. Wrong! There are some outstanding leaders coming through the system. Leaders that have the potential to take your organisation and the world to a fantastic future. Amazing people who will change the world—if they are given the opportunity. Kids who can learn more and learn it faster than you ever dreamed possible. Generation Y managers have the potential to turbo charge your business with new levels of energy, enthusiasm and intelligence. What you are saying when you say; "there are no good leaders on the horizon," is; "there are no leaders *like me* coming through the system."

I often hear people talk about their mentoring program and how they've mentored a young executive or professional to take over from them. Mentoring can work, but only if you can get past the first two letters... ME! Succession planning is not about you, it's about them.

This is the real succession planning problem. The current leaders are looking for people to replace them, not to succeed them and be greater than they are.

For your business to succeed, the next generation must be different and better than you. They have to be. You don't want another leader like you, you want one who is better than you.

"Better than me?" I hear you say agog. Think about it. We know that in the future technology, communications, transport, information and all other areas of life will be smarter, faster, better. You want your company to be part of this smarter, faster, better world and even lead it.

So how can you achieve this if the next generation of leadership is not smarter, faster and better than the current generation? Look at the word... <u>SUCCESS</u>ION. It tells you what it's all about. The aim is to succeed, not copy, duplicate, replicate or even dedicate. It's all about ensuring the long-term success of the company by ensuring the future leaders are smarter, stronger, faster and better. Like the six-million-dollar man, only with a suit and tie and a smart phone.

There are some amazing young leaders coming through, young leaders who can change the world, your business, and even you if they get the chance. Give it to them!

The entire world is built on the *Theory of Evolution*, i.e. that each generation will be better than the one that preceded it. Darwin could have written a decent leadership book because he understood that for any species to survive, and thrive, it is essential that successive generations evolve.

When you think about it that way, ensuring the next generation of leaders is better than you is just the natural way of things.

3. An inability to communicate across successive generations. There are three truisms about each successive generation:

- Every generation has its own language, clothes and music.
- Every generation believes that their generation is right, and those that came before and after are wrong.
- Every generation does not communicate effectively with those that came before and after.

We all try to communicate across successive generations, but the only word that seems to work across all ages from all eras is 'cool'. And even though what's 'cool' to one generation is not 'cool' to the next, we all seem to understand what 'cool' is.

Some of us pretend to like the music and clothes of other—usually younger generations—to hang on to our own disappearing youth and increasing 'un-coolness'. Some of us pick up a few of the latest words, phrases and sayings of the next generation to convince them we are "one of them" instead of an increasingly fogey-ish old fogey. But rarely do we communicate with another generation with trust, respect and humility.

And that's a big problem. By not listening to or understanding the next generation how can we hope to provide them with the opportunities they need to lead, to discover their potential, and ensure the sustainable success of the world?

The next generation is capable of learning faster and learning more than any previous generation. In fact, the next generation may well accelerate the rate of knowledge growth in the world, and in doing so, take every industry and every walk of human endeavour to new, exciting and never-dreamed-of places.

The capacity to connect with other generations is a quality to be prized, valued and fostered. The ability to connect with the wisdom and experience of a previous generation while being able to connect with the energy, passion, enthusiasm, creativity and learning potential of the next generation is one of the greatest gifts any human being can possess.

4. A lack of real responsibility.

You only have to read a newspaper, listen to a radio news program, or watch the TV news to see how this leadership failure has hurt the world. The economic issues the world is facing, the corporate collapses, the business bankruptcies and exploding enterprises can all be linked to one core problem: no one—no corporate leader or politician or academic—is prepared to accept real responsibility.

We have presented people with leadership, given them the freedom to lead, even taught them how to lead, and, if or when they have failed, we have rewarded them for it. CEOs, company directors and board members all get big payouts and large bonuses regardless of the actual performance of the organisation.

The phrase performance bonus is inappropriate and inaccurate these days. It should be the "you'll get rich no matter how poorly you perform or how badly your leadership screws things up", bonus.

No species, no organism, no nothing in the history of the universe has ever rewarded chronic failure. Just tell the dinosaurs, the dodo, the makers of Betamax video recorders and the

Tasmanian tiger it's ok to fail as you will still be eligible for a long, happy, successful future and species survival.

The last person across the line in the Olympic 100 metres doesn't get the gold medal. The team that loses the Super Bowl doesn't get the Champion's Ring.

In life, there are winners and there are losers and there's a cost and a responsibility for both of these imposters.

Responsibility is the cost of leadership: one can't exist without the other. They go together: fish and chips, salt and pepper, government and taxes, pizza and anchovies, leadership and responsibility.

Look at the messages we are giving the next generation of leaders. "It's OK to lead, to take risks, to make bad policy and poor decisions and fail, and if you do fail, the government will gift you a big bailout package and you will still get to lead, to get a big bonus and to go on failing."

Never in the history of leadership have we accepted leadership without responsibility—and it is a fundamental reason things have gone pear shaped. It's all about people, potential and performance.

5. Finding and keeping great people—gain, train and retain.

Many of today's corporate leaders lament the difficulty in finding or retaining quality people. Rubbish. The number one reason you believe you can't find and retain great people is that the people applying for positions have changed. They are not looking for you to give them a job for life—they are looking to give life to your job!

The old recruitment retention model of bringing someone in, putting them in a pathway to progress and expecting a lifetime commitment to the company is dead and buried. People want to join an organisation, use the people, position, platform and possibilities to speed up their career pathways, then, a few years later, move on to another company, another role or even another career.

Think about people differently. In the old days, we recruited people and asked them to commit to a lifelong relationship with the company where they would spend years playing the specific roles the company determined they needed to play. We used to think of people as machines, like equipment—'laptops with legs'. We recruited people to become part of the furniture.

Now, people are like fuel. They are like those funky new energy drinks—take a few in and keep your organisation dancing all night Talented people join organisations not to become part of the furniture but to become the fire and energy and desire and driving force of the company.

So, if people come to you with fire in their eyes, passion in their belly and drive in the hearts, and you offer them the nice office in the corner instead of listening to them, understanding their needs and providing them with the stimulating opportunity they crave, it's no wonder you can't find or keep great people.

Imagine for a moment that your employees are your clients. The client says; "I need you to listen to what I have to say.

I need to have the opportunity and the environment to explore my potential, to be engaged in decision making, to speed up my rate of learning and development and to challenge myself and grow as a human being every day." And you say to the client; "That's great, but this is the way we do it here." The client will not buy what you have to sell.

Imagine your current and potential employees are buying products and services from you. A customer walks into a store and asks for a state-of-the-art laptop. The salesperson says, "No that's not what you want. You need a dishwasher." No sale.

A hungry kid walks into a candy store and says; "Can I please have a box of Gummi Bears?" The store owner replies; "You don't want those. You want marshmallows. They're my favourite." No sale.

A young lady walks into a hairdressing salon and says; "I would like a shampoo, colour, condition and style please." The stylist suggests; "That's not what you need. You need a total shave—bald would really suit you."

An intelligent, motivated, talented Gen Y-er or Gen-I-er walks into your HR department and says; "I am here to learn, grow and become the best I can be." And the HR manager says; "Here are our rules, our policies, your KPIs, your leave entitlements and remuneration details." No sale.

Story time...

One of my great mentors was the legendary swimming coach Forbes Carlile. Forbes' revolutionised swimming and coaching with his innovative thinking, dogged determination and relentless pursuit of improvement in everything he did.

I would often call him and ask him his views, argue with him about ideas and seek his wisdom. On one occasion while I was working with the Australian swimming team I thought I'd come up with an incredible new idea—something that would revolutionise the sport and give the team an advantage leading into the Olympic Games.

After several months of hard work and research into this idea, I rang Forbes and told him all about it. I was so excited to share my "brilliance" with my old friend and mentor. Forbes said; "I'm going to send you something in a few minutes. I want you to read it and then call me back."

A short while later, I sat reading the material Forbes had sent me. I was stunned. It was a copy of a newspaper article from the early 1960s. There was a photo of Forbes on the deck of a pool in Sydney demonstrating the idea that I had 'invented'—only he had invented it over forty years earlier.

I rang him.

He said; "You can't see the future until you understand the past. You need to know what's come before you in order to lay a clear path in front of you. Being innovative is not just thinking, saying and doing things YOU haven't done before…. it's about thinking, saying and doing things that NO-ONE has done before and you'll only know that if you do your homework. Being a leader means having a two-way vision: seeing both the past and the future with absolute clarity."

LESSONS IN NOT LEADING—WHAT DIDN'T YOU LEARN?

1. Succession planning means the next person must be better than you.

2. Communication is King. Connection is the Emperor.

3. We need a new type of leadership.

Chapter Five

What is this potential thing? And where can I buy some?

Imagine you are at a trade exhibition overseas. The biggest and best companies in your industry are all there talking about the things they've done and the equipment that has contributed to their success.

You see a new machine used by one of the leading companies in your industry that you believe will revolutionise your organisation and will increase your company's production and profitability to unheard of levels. You have to buy it. You must have it. You can't imagine life without it. Out comes the company credit card, which to your amazement can be used for something other than taxis, tickets, tolls and take aways—and you buy it— the "it" that will make your company number one.

It gets delivered. You plug it in. You decide not to read the manual or spend time understanding the full potential of the machine because you have been in the business for 20 years and have seen it all, done it all and know it all.

Then a funny thing happens—the machine doesn't live up to expectations. Because the machine never works at its full potential, you never realise the promised increased production and profits.

What would you do?
a. Get in a mechanic, electrician, engineer or designer and try to fix it and make it run more effectively?
b. Send it back and ask for a new one?
c. Scrap it and go back to what you have always done?
d. All the above?

You didn't read the manual. You didn't spend the time to understand how to best utilise the new machine or attempt to learn about its capabilities. This is why people don't perform. We don't read their 'manual' on how to help them work to their full potential. We hire them, plug them in and hope they get it right.

If they don't work as we had expected, we send them to the 'mechanic' for training programs, courses, workshops and activities in assertiveness, self-confidence, team development and our old pal... leadership training. And, if that doesn't work, we shift them up, left, right, down or out and start all over again with another 'machine'. Or, we go back to our old machines and ask them to work harder.

Pause for a second and think about this. Because something new and different didn't work to our expectations, we assumed something was wrong with it and tried to make it conform to what we wanted and expected.

There's a myth in sport (as there is in most industries) about how having the best facilities and the latest equipment is the key to success. Most people believe spending money on new things and on building new places will solve their performance problems.

I was working with a city on a potential Olympic bid. They asked me to do a facility audit—a review of the sporting facilities across the city to allow then to understand what they needed to build to host an Olympic Games. As part of the audit process, I visited each of the Olympic sports and asked them to list what they needed to ensure the city had world class sporting facilities. One sport had few athletes, a poorly designed athlete training program, coaches who had failed to produce success at international level over the previous 20 years and inexperienced, amateur, volunteers running their sport. They told me unanimously that all they needed was a world-class facility and they would soon become a leading international sporting team.

In reply, I said; "It's no good coming up with great solutions to the wrong problems. I believe new facilities will not make a difference to your performance because your old facilities are not the problem."

Regardless, the facility was built and ten years later they still have few athletes, a poorly designed athlete training program, unsuccessful coaches and poor management. They all just fail in a nice new facility.

Instead of changing the way we think or the way we work or our own expectations of what's possible, we assumed the new machine was broken and brought in a procession of people, programs and processes to try to fix it up. That's the problem right there.

Why do you hire people? So, you have a bunch of people to use the new coffee machine? So, you have a team of people to take home company stationary (c'mon you know we all do it)? So, you would have a group of people to help fill up the payroll manager's time? So, you've got some cool kids to dance with at the next company Christmas party? No.

You hire people to add value to the organisation: to enhance the performance of the organisation. You saw something special in them and wanted that special something to help grow your business. You realised your current systems, structures and operations have limitations, so you employed someone to help break the limits, challenge the rules and take you to a new level of effectiveness, efficiency and excellence.

The name of the game is potential. Everyone has close to unlimited potential—they just don't know it. Or they know it but they place limits on it. People place limitations on their own potential because of a lack of self-confidence, lack of self-belief and a lack of faith in themselves. Managers place limitations on people's potential by not allowing them to lead, express their uniqueness, or restraining the genius of their staff through the imposition of their own limitations. Organisations place additional limitations on people's potential by enforcing rigid systems, structures and policies.

So, if the employee has limitations and the managers have limitations and the organisation has limitations, who will help the organisation achieve its performance goals? Who will help the organisation realise and sustain its full potential?

It's like a sporting team with internal conflicts between players, coaching staff and management. How can you beat up the opposition if you are wasting time, effort and energy beating up each other? Or imagine a boxer in a world title fight who's sparring his opponent with his left hand while giving himself upper-cuts and crosses with his right hand.

Unless everyone is committed to being the best they can be and to providing the environment and opportunity for everyone to succeed, no one can.

Time to talk change.

Story time...

Physical Talent is over-rated in sport. Everyone goes looking for the biggest kid, the strongest athlete, the fastest runner, the tallest player, but it's not physical potential that determines success.

I was invited to spend time with the USA Swimming team leading into a major international swimming competition. The topic of potential came up in conversation with some of the USA swimming team coaches.

I asked; "What's the one critical, non-negotiable, must-have quality that all great athletes need to be successful?"

Almost unanimously the reply was commitment.

I thought about this for a moment and said; "OK. I agree with you, but there's a problem. We can coach athletes to be faster, to get stronger, to have better technique, to improve their endurance, that's easy, but how can you coach commitment?"

A coach who'd worked with some of the greatest swimmers the US had produced, including world record holders, world champions and Olympic gold medallists responded; "Simple. In any given situation, when given a choice between doing things the easy way or the hard way, a committed athlete will do things the hard way."

"Interesting concept," I replied. "But can you give me an example?"

"Sure," he said. "In the morning, when the alarm goes off... easy way—choose to hit the snooze button and go back to sleep. Hard way—choose to get up, pack your bag, eat a quick, healthy breakfast and head out the door to training. When you get home… easy way—open the fridge, eat whatever you like… chocolate, ice cream, cake, drink soda, and watch TV until late at night. Hard way—make a healthy nutritious meal, drink plenty of fresh clean water and get to bed early so you're refreshed for another day."

He continued; "Success is a choice. It's the cumulative effect of choosing to do things the hard way, or if you like, the right way, that makes all the difference. Talent by itself is over-rated. Potential does not guarantee success; however, athletes with potential who learn to make the right choices can be unstoppable."

LESSONS IN NOT LEADING—WHAT DIDN'T YOU LEARN?

1. People have unlimited potential.

2. Remove limits to your thinking and attitudes.

3. Invest in the potential of people first—then look at buildings, infrastructure and technology. A poor attitude in a brand-new office is still a poor attitude.

Chapter Six

Change, and why is it so tough to do it?

Change is one of the most talked about aspects of life. It is essential if you want to improve, realise your potential, and be all you can be. Everything worthwhile in life demands a commitment to some level of change. Nothing changes if nothing changes.

In every city across the globe there are countless people sitting around wishing, hoping and dreaming about what they want from life. More money, travel, a better job, a wonderful partner, a new car, a big house... wishes and hopes and dreams. But wishes, hopes and dreams are poor strategies for success.

It's only when people think about, talk about and act to make change that things happen. Nothing changes... if... nothing... changes.

But change is also one of the hardest things to introduce and sustain in any situation. Why? Because people who introduce change are often seen as radicals, rascals or ratbags.

One of history's greatest lessons is that people who take the lead in introducing new ideas, new inventions, new products, new philosophies, new ideologies and new thinking have to deal with numerous people who label anything new as silly, stupid and as something that must be stopped.

Change drivers and idea innovators have to fight through three phases of change management to make a real difference:

1. The Ridicule Phase

Real innovators, thought-leaders, lateral thinkers and change drivers have to first face the conservative thinkers who will label any push to change as stupid, ill-informed and ridiculous.

How often have you come up with an inspired idea, seen it with such passion and with such clarity you could almost touch it, taste it and smell it, only to have someone tell you; "that won't work here because we do it our way," or; "that's wrong because no one else does it."

So, what do you do when faced with that lack of enthusiasm for your new idea? You back down and you go back to doing what everyone else is doing (the safe option) how everyone else does it—and has always done it.

2. The Resistance Phase.

If the idea gets through phase one, it then meets harder and tougher opposition from people who benefit from the current way of thinking and who will fight to resist new ideas and any challenge to their position and beliefs. This is where it gets nasty.

3. The Righteousness Phase.

Finally, if you get through the days, weeks, months or even years of fighting, political manoeuvring, back stabbing, name-calling and other obstacles you have to overcome, you can introduce real change and ensure the organisation progresses.

And this is why change is so hard to implement. As most of us prefer popularity to performance and having coffee to having conflicts, we get to phase one, the ridicule stage, and go no further.

I was working with an athlete leading into an Olympics. She was well prepared, a talented athlete, a great trainer and a hard worker. She had, however, one serious problem with her technique. At training each day we would talk about it. Then we argued about it. Then we fought about it. Then we yelled and screamed about it. In the end, I decided her friendship was more important than any medal or victory and stopped fighting with her about it. I decided having breakfast with her and the team each morning was far more important (and much easier) than breaking the friendship.

Three months later, I had to sit and watch—and feel my heart break (and hers)—as her technique let her down when it mattered and she lost a certain Olympic gold. All because I compromised on the change process and chose mateship over medals.

There are two true but conflicting statements I can make about change:

Change is critical. Change is essential for survival. The faster you speed up your rate of change relative to your opposition, the more likely it is you will sustain competitiveness and win. *But…* organisations and most people are conservative. Some are so resistant to change they will resist it to the point of seeing the company fail rather than change their beliefs and their position. How can people defend this conservative thinking?

Success is a moving target. It's always been the same. Success is not a single destination or a permanent place. It's not a mountain to climb, as so many like to say it is. Success is merely a moment in time to reflect on what you've achieved and to think about how you can get even better.

I hate the phrase 'best practice'. People seem go looking for 'best practice' as if it's some fixed, final, absolute time or place or process—where the secret to success can be found. 'Best practice' exists only for a few moments. Once someone discovers 'best practice' they talk about it and post it to social media. And once other people find out about it, they'll figure out ways to make 'best practice' past-practice (well, the smart people will anyway).

Business leaders who are the first at designing, developing and delivering new products are the ones that change the world. They revolutionise what we do, what we think and how we live. Athletes, coaches and teams that introduce new ideas and innovations first are usually the winners, the champions, the gold medallists, the premiers - the success stories.

So, if change is the life blood of success, why are so many people so determined to open an artery and let the company bleed to death rather than embrace the change process?

There are two schools of thought about leading change:

1.   Change Livers (as in Live-ers—not the offal [awful] thing you eat with garlic and onions).
2.   Change Killers.

Change Livers are those people, with those ideas, words, and actions that give life to new ideas. Those people, those moments, those experiences, which scream *I can* and *I will*, and dream only of *what could be…* not what is. Those inspirational times when you see a remarkable, incredible, amazing future and it seems impossible that anything can stand in its way. Those magnificent days when you feel driven, motivated and energised by nothing more than a thought, a belief, a dream.

You know the people I mean. People who make you feel better just by them being in the room. People who infect you with happiness, joy, energy and enthusiasm. People who make you feel today is the day and now is the moment everything will be better.

Change Livers are people who give life to an organisation. They're the reason behind the success of outstanding organisations. They're the living, breathing force that drives performance in every field of endeavour.

Any organisation that seeks to gain and retain Change Livers will grow to be exceptional.

Being a Changer Liver has nothing to do with qualifications or experience or background. It's about them as human beings.

A friend of mine runs a large and profitable gymnastics club. She's got over 400 students and around 50 coaches and teachers. I asked her how she recruits new coaches and teachers. She replied; "By their smile." I joked; "What have their teeth got to do with being a great coach?" She said; "It's not about their teeth. It's about the way they make me feel. If they walk in to the interview and smile and I can feel their joy, their energy and their passion from that first moment, I give them a job—even if they've had no previous experience or are un-qualified. I am looking for people with a magic about them, who make a connection the first moment they meet you. I can train them to coach. That's the easy part. But I need people who make other people feel good right from the first moment."

And then there are Changer Killers: the people, the thinking, the words, the attitudes that stand in the way of change.

Let's look at some of the most common Change Killers.

"It's different here." The most common anti-change comment you hear when you try to change things is: "it's different here", meaning this organisation is different to the rest of the world and need not change, evolve or improve. Rubbish! Change is the one constant in the universe and if you believe your organisation need not change—what universe are you living in?

"You don't understand the culture of this company." While it's true all companies have a unique culture, what is also true is that the core principles of success apply to every organisation regardless of its culture. Culture is only a factor when that culture is conducive to consistent and continued success. Some organisations, sporting teams and people will fail year after year and still hang on to the current culture as some sacred relic that can never be challenged or changed.

"We don't have the money to change." Another common anti-change comment. After working with hundreds of organisations in 25 countries over the past 25 years, it's fair to say that money is rarely the issue. The most common impediments to effective change all have always been, and still are, personalities (i.e. people standing in the way of change) and politics.

"We're on top, so we don't need to change." It is harder to sustain success and repeat winning than it is to do it a single time; so logically, the people most in need of change are those who have been successful. However, often they are also the people most likely to believe they have hit on the 'secret formula to success' and will resist change harder than any group.

"That's not the way we do it here." A painful, destructive mindset that often permeates when board members, executives and management believe the solutions to the organisation's current problems lie in going back to the past. This is a real killer. Nothing has ever gone faster going backwards (except in the sport of rowing).

"You've never been a part of this industry, so you don't understand it." There is no doubt that people who understand the specifics of an industry can add significant value to the quality of leadership, but rejecting the ideas, suggestions and expertise of anyone who hasn't spent 20 years 'earning their stripes' is a guarantee of failure. It's like saying only musicians can appreciate music or that only artists can go to art galleries.

"We need to introduce change slowly." A great idea… if you want to improve slowly and let your competition get away from you.

"We have this dominating, hard headed, old chairman who refuses to change. We will never get anything going." Guess what? There is one of these in every company, in every country in the world. The 'old stager' who has been in a position for 30 years and will do anything to cling to power. Unfortunately, this is a fact of life—get over it, work around them and get on with it.

"I can't get people to buy into the need to change." Another fact of life. Ancient Greek philosophers have written about people's resistance to change—it is one constant in a universe that thrives on change.

"It's too difficult to change." No, it's not. Everyday things change. Technology. The way we eat. The way we travel. The way we communicate. Everything is changing and evolving. If you can't change, then you are out of pace with the rest of the Universe.

"No one else does it like that." But that's the whole point. The best time to introduce new ideas and new ways of doing things is when everyone else is doing the same stuff—the old stuff."

Think of the great people in business, sport, science, art and literature. Why do we admire and respect them? Because they were different and difference means change. Uniqueness is an advantage and leading change is a prerequisite for greatness.

We admire the firsts, the people who were the first ones to do something. The people who stood up and said; "There is another way of doing this." We admire the people who had a vision and did things differently.

Would you pay to go to a lecture or business seminar or attend a training course that advertised the guest speaker like this; "Come and see the guy who does what everyone else does and who is really good at telling you how to be like everyone else." Or, would you prefer to see someone who is new, different, unique and unusual. Someone who speaks boldly and bravely about the future directions and possibilities for your industry. Someone whose drive, determination and vision changed the way the industry operated. Someone who changed the way we think about doing business?

Change is uncomfortable for most people but it is an essential discomfort if you want to be successful, like buying a pair of jeans two sizes too small for a first date.

If you want things to change, be prepared to fight, fight hard, fight long but fight fair. Let the conservative thinkers in your company do the dirty stuff, the name calling and lie telling, just keep fighting a good, hard, clean fight and in the long run, you will win.

Change is like caring for the environment. Everyone knows it's important. Everyone knows something should be done about it. We all know we can't survive without it. As long as it is not me who is doing it. Change the world but let me have a 25-minute shower every morning, wear furs, throw litter in the lake and drive my V8 car to work.

Be yourself, be unusual, be different and be the first to try it another way. You'll feel better, and who knows, your way might just be the right way.

Remember when you were a teenager sitting around writing all that dark, bleak poetry and thinking; "Hey, I'm really different. I'm a unique person. No one understands things like I do," guess what... you were right. So, why did you give up on this personal commitment to uniqueness? Because an entire world told you you were not different, not special, not unique and to get on board the mediocrity train with the rest of us.

Be yourself, then back yourself. Do it your way. Make it happen and never give up. Change is difficult, but man is it worth it!

Story time...

Daring to be different can be one of the most challenging yet most rewarding experiences anyone can commit to.

I was working with a professional rugby team and one of the players did something extraordinary. He was the team's goal kicker and in a tight competition the extra points he could score for the team meant the difference between a great season and an average one.

He set himself a challenging goal: a target of kicking 90 percent of all goals he attempted over the coming year.

To achieve this, he made a personal commitment to kick 100 extra kicks at training each week. The team trained four times a week and after each training session, when the rest of the team had finished and were showering and changing, he would drag a large bin full of footballs onto the field and attempt 25 extra kicks, alone, with no other players or coaches.

At the first extra session, one of the other players yelled out; "Hey man, we're all heading out for dinner. Stop wasting your time kicking those balls and come out with us."

The practicing player smiled and yelled back; "I'll catch up with you guys later," and he went back to his task.

I watched him do his extra work once and counted the number of kicks he was doing.

1, 2, 3… 15,16, 17… 23, 24, 25, 26… 26?

I asked him during one of his practices; "What are you trying to do? Aren't you doing 25 extra kicks a session—100 extra kicks a week? I counted 26 kicks."

He replied; "Everyone thinks it's about doing more, about just doing extra. It's not. It's the way you do more that matters. It's not about counting kicks, it's about making every kick count. Twenty-five is only a number. I don't leave until I feel I've gotten better – and if that means 26 or 36 or 106, I don't care. It takes what it takes."

At the end of the year he'd 'failed'. He couldn't quite get 90 percent of kicks attempted. He'd only achieved 89.8 percent, but in doing so he helped the team to its best competition performance.

LESSONS IN NOT LEADING—WHAT DIDN'T YOU LEARN?

1. Change is critical for survival.

2. Most people know more about killing change than making it happen.

3. Change is the essential quality in sustainable success.

Chapter Seven

Changing culture - what is it and where can I buy some?

Culture: I always thought it was something scientists grew in a dish. Or it was the clothes, food and architecture of some far-off exotic destination. Or it was that club Boy George led in the '80s (Google it if you don't know what this means).

Apparently, every organisation has a culture—or at least every organisation wants a good one. I often get asked to work with an organisation to help create, build and grow a sustainably successful culture. This seemingly simple task throws up several challenging questions. What is this culture thing, anyway? What is a good culture? How do you create it, enhance it and change it? And, most importantly, what is your culture, where is it, what does it look like and who owns it?

I've been to several organisations that report to have a great culture. On closer inspection, however, most organisations that claim to have a great culture have one built on popularity, not on performance. They believe that because people get along with each other, play golf together twice a year, remember each other's birthdays and the names of all their co-worker's kids they have a fantastic, highly effective, successful, winning culture.

Believe it or not, the organisations in which everyone gets along are usually the ones that fail. Performance is not about remembering birthdays. (Although mine is May 21st—please send any gifts or money to the contact details at the back of this book). It's about creating an environment where people feel confident to express their originality, individuality and uniqueness openly and honestly and are able to unleash the full extent of their potential in a situation of respect, integrity and honesty.

Over and over clients tell me they've got a great culture when all I see is a bunch of blokes in nice suits who play golf together twice a year, a group of managers who have coffee every Tuesday, and an organisation that is more committed to not making waves than it is on achieving results.

I know one thing for sure, the way *not* to create is to bring in the culture change expert and hold the ubiquitous 'mission statement' workshop.

Don't you hate the old mission statement/values/vision day. You know the one I mean. It goes something like this... Someone at the organisation, (usually someone from human resources using the '*How to create winning organisations guide book*', which was probably written by someone who owns a company which develops mission statements) decides culture change is needed. (An HR department is a bit like your laptop at home—everyone has one but no one is sure how to use it to its full potential so we usually just buy one and leave it alone and hope it will work properly when we need it to).

"What we need is a break-out day where we all get together in the spirit of co-operation and team work and change the culture of the organisation," says a motivated and enlightened HR manager—usually after a few too many cold beers, red wines and ports over a long lunch with the CEO.

They enlist the services of a consultant with a nice suit, a perfect smile and more energy than a nuclear power plant, who gets the staff together in a big room, plays an ice breaker game or two, then says something like; "OK gang, what do we stand for? What do we as a group stand for? What is our trade mark? What do we want other people to think about us?"

Then, for the next 30 minutes, people yell out things like honesty, integrity, team work, passion, fun, service, quality and customers. Then the words are grouped together, a sentence, a 'mission statement' is formed, and hey, ho presto, abracadabra, the culture changes!

"Our honesty, integrity and team work will be consistently delivered with passion and fun to create service quality experiences for our customers"— (by the way, if you are thinking of using this MMS—Mock Mission Statement please send me a cheque for $25,000 first).

Let's face it, some people have been through so many of these sessions they end up yelling out what they know the executive and management want to hear. Admit it, you've played the "I am going to yell out the best and most important sounding words so that everyone thinks I am really cool" game, haven't you? We all have.

It's time we all faced the fact that the mission statement workshop thingo does not work and, most importantly, the behaviour and performance of the staff *does not change*—well, not for more than a few days, anyway. Be honest. When was the last time you did one of these all-day mission statement time-wasters and got a real, meaningful, sustainable, long term, relevant change in your organisation's culture? When did you last do a retreat in the mountains or some similar idyllic setting with a performance consultant and, as a direct result, saw a significant, measurable improvement in your products and services?

Culture does not change like this. Culture change comes because of a real commitment by real people to sustainable success, continuous improvement and performance enhancement. Culture grows from within people.

The mission statement thing is supposed to be about giving people the illusion of ownership over the philosophies, attitudes, direction and leadership of the organisation. But it is just that—an illusion. As real as honest politicians, low fat chocolate ice cream that tastes like full cream chocolate ice cream and taxi drivers without strong opinions on football and politics.

Culture spreads like a kind of positive virus. It feeds on enthusiasm. It thrives on passion. It seeks opportunities to learn and improve to sustain itself. Like a virus it needs to seek new hosts to help it grow and survive.

Culture is not a mission statement or set of words, it's a way of life! Culture comes from *consistency*—the consistent desire of people (and organisations) to perform. And more importantly, culture change is driven by actions and behaviours: by people making a serious commitment to changing what they do and how they do it.

I once worked with a football team who did the old mission statement bit *every year* with each new group of players, coaches and staff. We got all the usuals; honesty, integrity, humility, sincerity, mateship, fun, team work, passion, enjoyment, etc. We developed a lovely little vision statement; "We will work together to strive for excellence on and off the field in an environment of quality, consistency and fun." (sound familiar?)

Then when they hit the gym or the training paddock, the old behaviours came back; poor performance, inconsistent effort, substandard attitudes, and lack of commitment.

The actions bared no resemblance to the words. The behaviours did not support the vision. The culture did not change, the team's performance did not improve, the coach got sacked, the CEO retired and five years later, they are still trying to change the culture through the annual mission statement pilgrimage.

There is a better way! Instead of getting everyone together to yell out their favourite words and catch phrases, start with a small core of people—or even one person—who want to change. The desire to change is the critical element in the culture change equation.

Aim to understand who they are and what they want out of their lives. Spend quality time learning about them and how they work, what motivates them, what they want out of the organisation and what they have to contribute to its sustainable success. Then teach them how to maximise their own individual performance, their unique potential and how to work as a highly effective team. Teach them to teach. Teach them how to inspire and how to lead. Teach them to coach. Teach the art of inspiring change through emotional connection. Teach them to listen and understand before trying to be understood. Give them permission to be different. Give them the authority to be themselves.

'Authentic' leadership has become a buzz word (although I thought only bees used buzz words). Authentic leadership is nothing more than being yourself and being comfortable to lead yourself and others by thinking, saying and doing things representative of the real you.

Want authentic leadership in your organisation? In your team? In your school? Give people permission to be themselves and support them every day in every way to be comfortable being who they are in everything they do. Then provide the core group of 'authentics' with the environment and opportunity to 'infect' and influence other members of staff. Empower them to engage their team mates to learn and to grow. Empower them to drive the change process and the culture dynamic.

Nothing *enforced* is sustainable.

Nothing *imposed* creates continuous excellence.

Culture *grows* from within.

Story time...

I had the very great honour of working with one of the leading college swimming teams in the USA. The team had already demonstrated their quality by winning the NCAA (National College Athletic Association) Division One title.

The head coach, an outstanding and very experienced coach, asked me to talk to the team and suggest ways they could improve. This is always a challenge. Most of the time as a performance consultant you get asked to work with athletes and teams who are struggling and who are in need of help. It's rare to get the opportunity to work with a group at the top of their game, and to get the opportunity to help them get even better.

I observed the team for a few days and talked to the coach about what I saw. He then scheduled my talk with the team for the afternoon before practice.

The team gathered in the locker room and I sat in front of the group. I said, "I want to thank you for the opportunity to watch you over the past few days. It's been a great honour to see you guys in action and it's easy to see why you are the best swimming team in the world right now. You work hard. You're talented. You give everything you've got in everything you do. But I believe you can be better."

They leaned forward... just a little.

"You need to love each other more," I said. And they leaned back!

"Let me explain," I continued. "People who don't understand performance think being a great team means saying all those things you're supposed to say, yelling out all those little phrases like 'well done' and 'great work' and doing all the high fives and all that stuff. That stuff is easy to do but more importantly—it doesn't make any difference to performance. People who want to be the best want honest, direct and sometimes—if needed—hard and challenging feedback. They want to be in an environment that fosters excellence through continuous improvement and by working with people who will not only offer encouragement, but who will challenge them to be better—even if that means confronting each other about attitudes and behaviours that are holding them back from achieving their potential. This is where LOVE comes in.

The more you care about your team mates—to the point you want their success as much as they want it themselves—so that the team is by nature selfless and everyone knows advice and feedback is given with a clear commitment to team excellence and individual achievement.

If you create an environment where people can be tough on each other but it's done with respect and with the goal of helping individuals, and, the team as a whole, be brilliant—the more powerful the team environment can be."

LESSONS IN NOT LEADING—WHAT DIDN'T YOU LEARN?

1. Culture—you have to live it to make it real.

2. It's about setting standards and keeping to those standards without compromise every day, every day, every day, every...

3. Do what you always did—get what you always got. You have to change yourself to change the culture and change the result.

Chapter Eight

Systems provide consistency...but they do not produce greatness

Many of the world's great companies have outstanding systems. McDonald's systems mean you can buy a Hamburger in Athens that tastes the same as one bought in Adelaide, and fries purchased in London look, smell and taste the same as fries purchased in Las Vegas (believe me I've tried and my waistline is the all the evidence McDonald's needs to prove their system works).

Like a lot of kids, I worked for McDonalds when I was 17. I thought the little hats were cool, I got free burgers for lunch and it gave me enough pocket money to impress girls. I started as a bun man, then became a grill man, then even had a little crack at shift leader-man. I thought I was pretty cool in those days—a kind of rock star but with acne, fries and a coke. While I've changed over the past 30 years, the McDonalds systems based on simplicity, repetition, communication and consistency have stuck with me. When I am running the barbecue for the Mc-kids at home I still feel the old Mc-habits coming back when I am cooking their Mc-dinner.

Automobile companies, airlines, IT groups, furniture manufacturers, food producers, toy companies, communications companies... everyone is into globalisation, which necessitates standardised systems for product consistency.

Systems provide one thing above all—*consistency*. Systems provide a highly ordered, structured, standardised, uniform environment to deliver consistent products, people and profits. They provide company boards, management and shareholders some level of control and certainty over the quality of their products and thereby consistency in their share prices. In short, systems are a 'risk-management' technique that ensures everything and everyone, everywhere in the organisation thinks, says and does the same things.

Why do companies rely on systems? Because they all believe that...

Systems provide *consistency Consistency* develops *culture Culture* develops *sustainability*

Systems give a degree of confidence to the organisation's leaders that the quality of their products and services will be maintained with high integrity and consistency everywhere they are sold.

However, greatness is *unique.*

Greatness is *different.*

Greatness is *typically… atypical.*

Think of the greatest people in your industry. The thought leaders. The change drivers. The innovators. The ones who changed the direction of the industry in some way. Why do we call them great? *Because they are different!*

They see things, do things and create things that are unique and take the industry to new levels and in new directions. They break rules. They defy conventions. They take risks by trying new ideas. They do not accept boundaries. They ignore limits. They see the best of the present as only the starting point for the future. They... lead.

Systems do not create genius. Systems are designed to produce consistent quality and standardised outcomes, but they do not create real leaders or real winners. They are slow to respond to change and rarely provide industry leadership in innovation, quality or excellence.

Anson Dorrance the great USA soccer coach once said: "We are poor at recognising genius. Some kid comes along who has had limited training but they have a natural ability to score goals, beat opponents and see the game differently. They are potentially the next Messi or Maradona or Ronaldo.

"So, what do we do? We immediately put limits on them. We teach them to pass. We teach them to defend. We teach them to conform to our own philosophies about the game. We kill off their genius by putting barriers on them. We make them become part of the system—our system.

"Instead, we should be learning from them. Great players take the game to new levels and we should not restrain their genius by imposing our own limited views of what the game should be."

This is also true of companies that spend a lot of money finding the right people, then immediately put them into an internal training program to force them to act like, think like, move like, behave like everyone else in the company—to follow the 'company way'.

Systems are all about *what*—they teach *what to do* to ensure consistency. Genius is about *how* and *why*—really talented individuals do things differently, they take chances, they take what is known and challenge it with the unknown.

The ability to *recognise and nurture* genius is critical for your business to succeed. Think about it. You want our business to be unique, to have a point of difference from your competitors. You want to be special. You want to be seen as one-of-a-kind.

But then you try to develop a one-of-a-kind business by putting rigid systems and structures in place that limit your ability to be one-of-a-kind. You put in place policies and processes, which everyone in the organisation must learn and follow religiously because it is 'the system'. In doing this, you immediately stifle the genius and creativity inside your people. You put systems first, people second and eventually, as a result, clients last.

The same principle applies in business (talented managers and staff), in sport (talented athletes and coaches), in education (talented students and teachers) and even in families (talented children): stay true to the systems and culture that make you unique *but* empower, encourage and embrace talented people and give them an environment that provides them with the opportunity to realise their full potential. Do this and the rewards for you, for them and for the organisation are limitless.

A client recently mentioned they were having problems retaining quality staff. She ran a large company with over 150 branch offices across the nation. The biggest issue was that branch managers were leaving within their first year, costing the company millions in lost time in recruiting, advertising and so on.

A quick look over her exit interview statistics showed the answer. Managers commented that while the money, the job and the conditions were generally competitive, the biggest issue was the rigidity of the systems and policies they were expected to adhere to. Managers were learning the company's systems within a few months of being in the role, but then wanted to personalise them and be a bit creative with some aspects of them. The national leadership had a zero-tolerance policy on changes to the system or flexibility within the network, so any managers with talent, innovation, creativity and energy soon became bored and resigned. The company missed an opportunity to grow, change and perform by tapping into the leadership skills of their talented young branch management team. The one thing that could have transformed the company and turned it into a highly successful, industry-leading organisation—talented, creative, motivated leaders across their national network—is the very thing they destroyed.

By all means, create quality systems that give your organisation the consistency it needs to sustain competitiveness and produce consistently high-quality products and people, but understand your real edge comes from embracing change, from recognising *genius* and providing it with an environment to grow, flourish and ultimately add value to your systems and structures.

Learn to respect difference. Learn to embrace uniqueness. Learn and grow from watching genius and the atypical. Do not limit genius with your own limitations and paradigms. Don't put genius inside a box and restrain it. The only thing that will increase if you insist on sticking to rigid rules and stifling systems is your staff turnover.

So, what do people really need?

Story time...

One of the worst phrases in sport is, "If it ain't broke, don't fix it". This suggests the key to success is finding *the* way—the *only way* of doing things, then to keep doing it.

Human beings by nature seek *the* one way—the one method or technique or system that will guarantee success… and of course—it doesn't exist. There's never only one way.

I've had the opportunity to spend time with the New Zealand Rugby Union High Performance Unit and to learn from some of their outstanding coaches, including World Cup winning coaches Sir Graham Henry and Wayne Smith. Both coaches are very different in their philosophies and approaches, except in one area… their core commitment to one ideal… 'getting better never stops'.

The British and Irish Lions had just completed a tour of New Zealand, and the All Blacks had been at their most brilliant best… winning all three test matches.

Sir Graham and 'Smithy' invited me to come over after the tour and challenge the New Zealand High Performance Rugby coaching community to get better. A strange request given they'd just achieved a remarkable feat in defeating the mighty Lions.

So… I stood up in front of the entire New Zealand Rugby Union coaching community and said: Thank you the invitation to be here. Congratulations on your recent success against the Lions. What a remarkable achievement. However, the real goal—winning the Rugby World Cup is two years away. And… to be blunt… you've been here before. You've done remarkable things and been heralded as the best team in the world in the past. And…

you've failed. You've lost when it really mattered—in the Rugby World Cup. So, the question you've got to ask is not "why are we so good?", but "why do we continue to fail on the sport's biggest stage?"

The expression 'you could hear a pin drop' is relevant here. There wasn't a sound to be heard. Nothing.

Sir Graham—sensing a lynching was about to happen—stood up and said; "He's right. We've been here before. We've been in this room and all congratulated ourselves and told ourselves how good we are, and then we lose the one game that really matters. If we don't keep getting better, we'll do it again, we'll fail under pressure and the World Cup will elude us. Well, it's not going to happen while I'm in charge."

And I completed the rest of my session.

This is typical of outstanding leaders and great performers. No matter how good they are they know success is fleeting. They understand repeating success is much more difficult than achieving it the first time because once you've experienced success, the things that got you to the top—hard work, discipline, commitment, dedication, innovation, drive, purpose, resilience and passion, are either gone, or at the very least decreased. So, unless you've got a serious commitment to continuous improvement and are self-aware enough of your strengths and weaknesses, then repeating success is unlikely.

LESSONS IN NOT LEADING—WHAT DIDN'T YOU LEARN?

1. Systems do not create greatness.

2. Uniqueness is the key to leadership—be yourself.

3. Don't eat too much take away food.

Leading Without Leading

Chapter Nine

Finding and retaining the right people: real needs

A quick glance through the business and employment sections of any metropolitan newspaper will reveal two current problems in the corporate environment: it is difficult to find talented, experienced and qualified staff, and, it is difficult to keep them as talented people can shop around for better deals.

The four most important tips about attracting and retaining good staff are:

1. It's rarely about money
2. It's rarely about money
3. It's rarely about money
4. Read first three tips again

The trick is knowing the difference between the *market value* of the person's skills, experience and abilities and their *real needs value*.

The market value of a prospective or current staff member is easy to determine. A few calls around your network, a bit of research on industry websites, a little benchmarking and you can come up with a financial value for most positions in the workplace. Market value is all about money and commercial worth.

Real needs value is what it will cost to provide the person with a package and an environment which meets their real needs. Real needs value is all about *understanding* the real needs of the individual.

A football team I was working with in the USA were desperate to sign a talented young player. The player had attractive financial offers from several teams. We calculated his market value at $825,000—plus a maintained brand-new motor vehicle, a range of benefits for the player and his family, and the usual performance bonuses. If he had a great season, he could earn close to $2M a year.

I did some homework on the player's real needs and found out:

He enjoyed fishing.

He had three children under the age of seven.

His wife was a teacher who loved her job.

He was close to his parents.

So, the final offer to the player became:

Playing contract—$825,000.

Maintained motor vehicle (sports sedan)—value $70,000 per annum.

Second maintained motor vehicle (wagon with baby and children's seating installed)—value $50,000.

A small aluminium fishing boat—value $35,000.

Day care places guaranteed for all three children (including screening and assessment of day care centre)—value $45,000 per annum.

Three-day-a-week teaching position for his wife at a school located two-minutes' walk from home—value $40,000 per annum

Five return flights per year for his parents to come and visit, including accommodation and the use of a car when they are in town—value $25,000.

The player signed the contract within 24 hours of receiving it!

To steal a line from the famous Mastercard ad, "Cost of the player to the organisation $1M and change—value of showing how much the organisation valued the player as a person and would work hard to ensure the player and his family were happy, content and supported... priceless."

In this employment market—particularly with the Generation Y and I applicants—potential candidates are interviewing you as much as you are interviewing them. They are looking for organisations that offer more than a few extra dollars, a nice parking space and some extra days off for birthdays and special events. They are looking for opportunity, respect and an environment which satisfies their broader needs. They are looking for an organisation which "seeks first to understand, then to be understood!"

The funny thing is most companies ask questions about family, hobbies, sporting interests etc. at the bottom of their application forms when screening potential applicants.

The one part of the application form that tells you who the applicant really is, and therefore provides you with insights on what's motivating them, what inspires them and how to gain and retain them, should be at the top of your recruitment paperwork, in bold letters and highlighted in 26 different colours.

How many companies refer back to the same forms in the contract negotiation process to gain an insight into the REAL NEEDS of the applicant and put together an unbeatable offer?

"I don't care how much you know... I want to know how much you care" (Forbes Carlile)

The critical issue is to understand what inspires and motivates people.

Story time...

As part of the Australian Triathlon team preparing for the Olympic Games you get to spend time in some amazing and beautiful parts of the world. One of the most special places I've ever worked with a team would have to be in the South of France around Annecy and Aix Les Bains.

As team leader, it is essential to keep two things in mind at all times:

1.   The functioning of the team, i.e. the team being the coaches, the athletes, the physiotherapist, the massage therapist, the sports scientists, the nutritionists and team management.

2.   The happiness of each individual in the team.

These considerations are closely connected.

I have a habit of being extremely forensic (some would say nosey) about the people I work with in high performance environments. I am going to ask them to give more than they've ever given to anything in their lives, to work hard together, work early in the morning, to be away from home for extended periods, and to perform at their best when they're tired, stressed, fatigued and under pressure. In these situations, it pays to know who you're working with.

One thing I've learnt is to have a 'feel good box' full of stuff that has meaning to each of the individuals in the team to be used if and when needed. For example, on one tour one of the athletes was a mum and being part of the team and chasing her Olympic dream meant being away from her young child for an extended period.

One day she was particularly down and flat and missing home. When the athlete went out to train, we went into the 'feel good box' and pulled out a huge stack of pictures and drawings her son had done. We then proceeded to stick them up all over the walls of her room. We also had a short video of her husband and son telling her how amazing she was and how proud of her they were.

When she returned from training, there was her room covered in those crayon masterpieces and the video ready to play on. You can imagine the difference this made to her. She went on to have a wonderful Olympic experience.

It doesn't take much to build an environment based on genuine care and consideration for the people you work with, but it can be the most wonderfully rewarding experience of your life.

LESSONS IN NOT LEADING—WHAT DIDN'T YOU LEARN?

1. People are not just employees—they are human beings.
2. People have a wide range of needs—not just money.
3. People are motivated by different things at different times.

Chapter Ten

Motivation... ain't no such thing

Consultants, management experts and life coaches are always talking about motivation and some make lots of money doing motivation talks, motivation lectures, giving motivational speeches, writing motivational books, selling motivational videos, running motivational courses and generally being motivational! I feel motivated just writing this last paragraph. Please pause here while I go out for a run, join a gym and lose 50 kilos—I think I motivated myself a little too much in that first paragraph.

OK—I'm back. We can continue.

Here's the funny thing: motivation—there's no such thing—well at least not in the traditional sense. We've always believed motivation is something a leader or speaker or presenter or role model with a story to tell could give to other people. Here's the scoop, it doesn't work! No one can motivate anyone to do anything.

Motivation must come from within. Motivation is like a flame… it's burning—sometimes brightly, sometimes only flickering—inside the hearts and minds of every human being on the planet. It's a dream, or a hope, or a wish, or a passion, and it's there… somewhere, often just smouldering away, inside us all.

Then, when the time is right, or the right person or situation presents itself, or the opportunity arrives, it's like throwing fuel on that flickering fire and *pow!* it bursts into an explosive flame that drives people towards achieving remarkable things.

Everyone has a dream. To be happier. To be thinner. To be a better parent. To be a great leader. To marry a super model. To be healthy. To win an Olympic gold medal. To do all the above… "Maybe if I got healthy, I would be thinner, I would win an Olympic gold medal and get wealthy from endorsements, which would make me attractive to super models, we'd get married have kids, which I would lead effectively, and then I would be happy."

What most of us lack is the commitment to make our dreams a reality. The dream is the key, and the dream is the motivation. It is our desire, our fire.

People enlist the services of a motivator to inspire them with new ideas and to give them some direction in life, their careers or their sport. And many motivational speakers are great at presenting, telling stories of people who succeeded against the odds, people just like you who believed anything was possible and became successful, wealthy, a world record holder, etc.

So, typically you walk away from a motivational speech or motivation workshop feeling great… for about two days. That's because you never needed to go to a motivation lecture or workshop in the first place! Your dreams are your motivation and you have plenty of them inside you. The only motivator you need to listen to is yourself!

A motivator's real role is to provide the guidance, the systems, the structures, the technical knowhow, the knowledge, the skills and the support to help clients, athletes and others to find the discipline and commitment to turn dreams into reality.

Trying to motivate someone else is like teaching a pig to sing: it will frustrate you and annoy the pig.

So, an important lesson to all motivators—do not motivate. Encourage people to dream then help them engage the commitment to turn dreams into reality.

Then why do people lack the commitment to turn dreams into reality? Because other people keep telling them it can't be done. And other people keep putting obstacles in their way. Because other people keep telling them to stop dreaming and to do things the way they are.

When you go to school, you have to learn someone else's way. When you go to sport, the first thing you have to learn are the rules and how to play like everyone else. When you go to work, you have to do it someone else's way. For most of your life people tell you that your way needs to change to conform to someone else's way. And, after years of believing your way is not the right way, most of us end up accepting it and our dreams die as surely as our dress sense, taste in music, and management of excess body hair.

I was invited to do some corporate coaching with the owner of a top-100 company. He built the company up from nothing—an original backyard to brilliance story. At our first meeting, he told me his life story. His 'book' had all the usual 'chapters'. Chapter one: it started with a dream. Chapter two: I made a plan. Chapter three: I worked really hard. Chapter four: I had a lot of early setbacks. Chapter five: I had cash flow problems in the first few years. Chapter six: I persisted and things started to turn around. Chapter seven: people kept telling me I was foolish to try something new. Chapter eight: we kept working hard and eventually made some breakthroughs and secured some major contracts. All the essentials for a bestseller.

The thing that made the biggest impact on me however was his insight into his own life. "I was not very good at school. I got bored easily and was often the kid in class getting in trouble for talking and disrupting everyone else. I would sit in class dreaming about all kinds of stuff. Then when I wrote or spoke about my dreams in class, teachers would criticise me and tell me I was wrong because it wasn't what they thought or they believed or the way I was supposed to think. This happened so often I began to think I was dumb and there was something wrong with me. I failed my final year of high school and went through a succession of jobs, which I hated—all the time believing the aim of life was to fit in and to think like everyone else.

"It wasn't until I realised that I needed to learn my way, to think my way and to do it my way that things started to turn around for me. I went back to becoming a dreamer. But with one important difference, I became a dreamer with passion and a fire and a desire to see my dreams become real."

I wonder how many other kids who are a little different, or who do not learn the way they are supposed to learn, give up, stop trying, stop dreaming and go through life thinking there is something wrong with them? Or even worse, are given tablets and pills to force them to change the way they learn, act and behave?

How many people start life as creative, original, innovative beings but lack the support, love, guidance, opportunity and leadership at critical moments in their life and never realise their potential?

Get excited about other people's dreams. Get as excited about their dreams as they are. Maybe even more excited. Nothing is more infectious than enthusiasm. There is nothing more precious than passion. Nothing is more powerful and more energising than knowing with certainty you are surrounded by people who've got your back and who believe in you. Find ways to help them realise their dreams—even if their dream isn't yours. This is particularly true in helping and encouraging people to be the best leaders they can be.

Instead of backing our bosses, supporting our supervisors and lauding our leaders, we look for ways to bring them down (and maybe even take their jobs). This is so dumb—dumb, dumb, dumb, dumb.

Think about it. Leaders have a vision about the future. This is the fundamental difference between a leader and a manager. A leader thinks, talks, sees and believes in 'what could be'. They have a vision for the future. A manager deals with 'what is' and puts in place the systems, structures, routines and programs to bring that future to life. A vision is a dream someone is working hard to turn into reality. So, leaders are dreamers—like you.

The most common response we give when someone shares their dreams with us is to change their dreams to be more like ours. We try to change their dreams with supportive comments like:

"Hey, that's really great but you should be doing... "

"Good on you for having a dream, but the way things are done here is... "

"I used to think like that, but the reality is... "

"Hey that's a good idea but you should change it to... "

We can't wait for them to stop talking about their stupid dream—i.e. stupid in the sense it's not our dream therefore it must be stupid—so we can tell them about our dreams.

Imagine what a world, what a workplace, what a team you would have if instead of cutting down tall poppies you helped them grow taller. (Don't think I didn't see the opportunity to work a fertiliser comment into the analogy).

The smartest thing you can do is help leaders achieve their dreams, to encourage them to dream, and to dream along with them. This is precisely why the 'Ten Ways to be a Great Leader'—type of training program does not work.

Story time...

Every day I receive emails and messages through social media from parents, coaches and athletes asking me to do something motivational. Here's an example:

Dear Wayne,

My daughter needs your help. She's 15 years old and a really talented basketball player.

When she was eight, she was an outstanding basketballer. You would never see her without a basketball in her hands. She would bounce a ball everywhere she went—even slept with her favourite basketball.

t 10 everyone said she would one day make the Olympic team for basketball. When she turned 12 she was the state junior basketball program MVP (Most Valuable Player). Then, for some reason, it all changed when she turned 14.

She stopped wanting to go to practice. We had to force her to do any training. When she was younger, she would always be shooting hoops before and after school. Now she never wants to pick up a ball or train or play.

She's just turned 15 and wants to give up basketball. Can you please talk to her and motivate her to get back onto the court and become a great player?

Signed, Desperate Mum and Dad.

And here's my response:

Dear Desperate Mum and Dad,
Thanks for your email.

I do understand your dilemma and I can sympathise with the frustration you are obviously feeling right now. However, no, I will not motivate your daughter.

No one can motivate anyone to do anything they don't really want to do. Well—let's put that another way—no one can motivate someone to do something they don't really want to do and have that person do that something to the best of their ability.

You can force someone to do something they don't really want to do—or bribe them, or offer them incentives—but in the end, if the passion and the drive and the commitment to do it is not coming from inside of them, it's not going to work.

I've spent 25 years of my life working with some of most talented athletes and coaches all over the world and the one thing I'm certain of is that the best of them never need motivation… they never need it because they've already got it.

My advice is this. Let it be. Allow her time and give her the opportunity to decide what it is she really wants to do. If basketball is in her heart, and if somewhere in her heart the love of the game is still there, she'll come back to it. Maybe after a few weeks. Maybe after a few months. Maybe after a season or two, but if she loves the game, she'll come back to it.

If she doesn't come back, then let it go. Love her unconditionally for the wonderful, amazing, incredible young person she is and let her know whether she plays basketball, hockey, table tennis or takes up the Yo-Yo, it doesn't matter to you—that you as mum and dad love her unconditionally and value and accept her for who she is and not for what she does or doesn't do on a basketball court.

Sincerely,

WG.

LESSONS IN NOT LEADING—WHAT DIDN'T YOU LEARN?

1. Get motivated.

2. Be passionate.

3. Dream. Never stop dreaming.

Chapter Eleven

Ten reasons why "Ten Ways to be a Great Leader"—style books don't work

This wouldn't be much of a leadership book (even if it's about not leading) if it didn't have a list or two, now would it?

You could add up all the money spent on leadership books, downloads, podcasts, DVDs, CDs, training courses, training programs, leadership workshops, breakouts, retreats, boot camps and leadership conferences and use it to solve world poverty, find the cure for cancer, fly the entire population of Pakistan to Jupiter for a holiday and still have enough left to pave most of the major highways in the USA with solid gold.

Why do people all over the world have this obsession with learning to lead?

Because society tells us being a leader is a good thing. That's true. Because we want to learn to be better, to improve, to find a way to realise our potential. Yes.

Because we believe if we follow the leadership tips and tricks of great leaders we might also become great leaders and reap the benefits of leadership—money, political influence, fame, glory. No doubt.

Why keep looking out for answers? It was looking at you this morning in the mirror as you shaved (hopefully this only applies to the men and bearded ladies reading this chapter) and combed your hair. The fundamental reason everyone is looking for answers in leadership books and training programs is they lack the courage, faith, confidence and belief to look for answers in themselves.

The essence of leadership is difference, uniqueness, and the courage to be yourself and stand up for what you believe. Everything you ever needed to know about leadership is in these four words: be yourself, back yourself. You don't need leadership lessons, you need ME-dership lessons. (Wouldn't be much of a leadership book without a few quirky, made up words either!)

Leadership programs and books and courses all sour they should work and should be what you need, but what you really need to do is ignore them and instead focus on being who you are and not being afraid to think, do and say what you believe is right.

In the tradition of all the lists in all the great leadership books, here is the list of ten reasons things like lists about leadership don't work:

1. You are not Winston Churchill and shouldn't try to be. C'mon now admit it. How many times have you picked up a leadership biography and gone; "that's it, that's me. From this moment on, I will lead like Winston Churchill, or Kennedy, or Lincoln, or Bill Gates, or Phil Jackson, or Gandhi, or Wayne Bennett, or Kevin Sheedy, or Rod Macqueen, or the Dalhi Lama." These are all remarkable people, but they are not you and you are not them. Be yourself. You are remarkable.

2. Leadership models need a lot of glue to make them work. Every week someone comes out with the 'all new, all singing, all dancing' leadership model. Like all models, they are only as good as the people who build them and the quality of glue they use. And glue in the corporate sense is the commitment, attitude, passion and hard work of the people in the organisation. Models are only as good as the people who build them!

3. Times are changing faster than leadership models can keep up with. Leadership is about the future. Management is about the present. Education is about the past. Leadership is a dynamic, rapidly changing beast with no rules, no limits and no boundaries and it needs to change, evolve and respond rapidly.

4. You want leaders to be creative, unique, individual, innovative, unusual, original, eccentric, different, special, genius. How can we enhance this unlimited leadership thinking by sending people to courses with limits? For example; Nine Rules of Nine Great Leaders Leadership, the Ten Commandments of Leadership from the Cincinnati Bowling Alley Business School, the Five Golden Rules of Gold Medal Leadership. Leadership is not about a number or list of rules or prescription of power or set of order. In fact, by training leaders to follow the Eight Magic Universal Laws of the Leadership Universe, you are stifling the thing you are trying to create.

5. Leadership is big business. There are people making millions selling leadership programs, books, downloads, e-books, DVDs, videos, workshops, lectures, programs, courses, online training and one-on-one coaching contracts. It is in their interest to make everyone believe they—the 'leadership gurus'—have found the secret to leadership and without it, you will never reach your potential as a leader. It is impossible for the big leadership development groups to fit their product to each individual so they have to make the individuals fit the product. So, you have to go

through several set steps, stages, levels, phases and strategies to fit a specific commercial brand of leadership. Formula One cars (and drivers) do not come off a production line.

6. Learning to lead comes from doing. Because leadership begins and ends with you being yourself and understanding who you are, you have to experience life. Great leadership depends on wisdom. Wisdom can be defined as having great judgement, the ability to make the right decisions at the right time. And you only learn judgement through experience. Want to see the best leader you will ever meet? They were looking back at you in the mirror this morning. Want to read the best leadership manual (apart from this one of course), take an honest look at your own life, the lessons you have learnt and are learning every day.

7. Leadership is life. It's taken you a lifetime to become the person you are now. You are the sum of your experiences. No matter how good a leadership training program may be, a week in the bush hanging by your toes over a burning pile of coal while chanting; "I am good, I am great, I am wonderful", will not change 37 years of lacklustre leadership. Your leadership will change when you change and you will change when you accept the greatness of your uniqueness.

8. Books, courses and workshops teach 'what', they don't teach 'how'. And they don't teach how to make meaningful, real, sustainable change when you hit the tough times. And they don't

teach you about what's important to you, what you value and how to lead your own way.

9. They assume someone else must always know the answers: At 6a.m. every Monday, 1000 consultants leave New York for a week of consulting in Los Angeles. At the same time, 1000 consultants leave Los Angeles to work in New York for seven days. Now, the New York and LA consultants have the same stuff to teach but being from out-of-town gives them credibility, and the respective groups are lauded by their audiences as being innovative and possessing genius. The lesson is—genius might be living next door—have you bothered to listen? A really great way to stifle creativity, ingenuity and innovation in your own organisation is to spend thousands of dollars looking for new ideas in others. In the end, your own people give up trying to be creative and innovative and just give you the minimum standard, which in any business or performance focused environment, is suicide.

10. The *'who'* delivering the program is more important than *'what'* they are delivering. Ask yourself:
a. Does this person know this stuff?
b. Do they live this stuff?
c. Do they know anything about me?
d. Do they care about my dreams and my life?
e. Can they offer me something that, if I put my mind to it, I can't figure out for myself?

If you can answer yes to all the above, then maybe you can learn something from this person, course or program. If not, spend your time, money and energy on understanding yourself some other way.

There are lots of whacky leadership courses and programs out there, and I have been to most of them. But one stands out for the 'Golden knucklehead award' for outstanding leadership training. The facilitator had everyone on the course stand up and put a paper bag over their heads. We then had to walk around and bump into each other, chairs, tables, etc. The lesson, he said, was that leadership is like wearing a paper bag on your head. You keep bumping into things and you have to learn how to deal with them. Not that bad a message when you think about it. Only problem was he forgot to close the door of the training room and three course participants bumped into the top of the stairs and had to learn how to deal with two flights of stairs, a broken arm, a broken leg and various cuts and abrasions. Not only that but two of the learner leaders ended up wearing the 30 serves of quarter sandwiches, four large trays of fresh cut fruit and 10 litres of orange juice that was set aside at the back of the room for our lunch break. To you Mr X (you know who you are) leadership trainer extraordinaire—congratulations!

Course, clinics, coaching and conferences might provide ideas, inspiration, imagination and innovations but they don't absolve you from the critical component in successful leadership... personal responsibility.

Story time...

I am a big believer in developing unique learning experiences for each client based on their current specific needs rather than trying to sell them off-the-shelf, or one size-fits-all solutions to their problems. I am also passionate about working with athletes, coaches and teams 'in context', i.e. working with them on court, at the pool, at the track, in the gym and so on, to make the learning more relevant and real.

This bespoke approach doesn't always secure contracts as the majority of people seem to want to see an off-the-shelf product or program before they buy it.

I pitched for a performance enhancement program contract with a professional sport. After the pitch, they contacted me and advised that I'd been unsuccessful in securing the contract. As is my practice, I asked them where could I improve and where I lost the business.

They said, "The company that won the contract offered us proven, evidence-based methods to analyse the leadership qualities of our coaches, athletes and managers and have a seven-step program guaranteed to improve the performance of our team."

Around a year later, the same organisation contacted me and asked for a meeting. I asked, "How is your leadership program going?"

They responded, "We terminated the contract."

"Why?" was the obvious follow up question to ask.

"They didn't know the sport. Even after several months of being here, no one from the training company knew the names of any of the players or coaches. No one had ever attended a game or a training session. They even tried to get the coaches to change the way they coached to be more like the executives in other organisations they had worked with. They couldn't even remember the basic rules of the game and, what's more, they didn't even care. I guess you could summarise it this way: they tried to force our players and coaches to fit into their models rather than adapt their models to help us get better. They tried to get us to be the same as everyone else they had worked with rather than teach us how to be the best we could be."

LESSONS IN NOT LEADING—WHAT DIDN'T YOU LEARN?

1. Lists about leadership are meaningless.
2. Lists about leadership are meaningless.
3. Lists about leadership are meaningless.
4. Lists about leadersh…

Chapter Twelve

Ok, there's a catch, it's called personal responsibility

I've got four young kids. They all want to lead—that is, they all want the freedom and the environment to do things their way and to express their uniqueness. Our family life is a constant balance between providing the kids with the environment and opportunity to learn to lead with the parental instinct to ensure they do it in a supported, safe and secure environment.

So, I have a choice to make. I can…

1. Tell them they are too young and too inexperienced to lead

Positive: It is easier and safer for me to lay down Dad's law. That's the way I learnt and my dad learnt and his dad learnt and his dad learnt and his dad learnt and… you get the idea.

Negative: Wisdom is judgement—knowing what choices to make in different situations. And you don't learn how to make the right choices unless you have experience. So, if I deny them the learning experience they may never fully develop wisdom. (This is Dad's and most manager's biggest problem—we want our 'kids' to develop wisdom but we deny them the opportunity to develop it).

2. Give them some limited freedom and leadership

Positive: They get some experience but within my guidelines, my rules, my boundaries, framework and safety limits.

Negatives: They learn and grow by my rules and my views without truly expressing their uniqueness and understanding who they are. They become 'mini-Wayne' and the world is not ready for that.

3. Give them unlimited freedom and the opportunity to express their potential

Positive: They learn to be themselves and to learn the joy of trying new things and experiencing life.

Negative: Some things can be dangerous for very young kids. My two-year-old wants to drive my new Honda and my five-year-old wants to try skydiving (which, in itself is not bad but his version of skydiving is to do it off our veranda wearing nothing but a smile and a superman cape).

What do I want for my kids?
• To live a long happy life.
• To find their passion and follow it.
• To have confidence in themselves, to attempt anything—that fear of failure never be a barrier to them experiencing life.
• To enjoy learning and never stop growing as people.
• To laugh as often as possible.
• To be driven by their own values and what's important to them—i.e. to not allow themselves to be peer driven.
• To lead themselves.
• To realise their full potential and love every minute of exploring it.
• And—most importantly—to do it all better than me!

I do a lot of sport parenting education (i.e. educating the parents of kids who play sport). Over the past 25 years, I've spoken with thousands of parents all over the world about how they can better support their children through the experience of sport. One of the exercises I do with the parents is to have them close their eyes, take a few deep breaths and imagine it's ten years from now. "Imagine you are walking down a street, and there, coming the other way, is your son or daughter ten years older than they are today. You see them, and they see you. You walk towards each other. I want you to imagine you stop and talk with them for a few minutes. What do you see? What do you hear? What do you feel?" I then ask the parents to share their vision with other parents in the room. Over the past 25 years of doing this not one parent anywhere in the world has ever said; "I saw my son with an Olympic Gold medal around his neck", or; "I talked with my daughter as she stepped out of her new Porsche". What the parents 'see' is a big smile on their future-kid's face and they experience a warm feeling of love and kindness. The things that have the greatest value in life cost nothing.

As a dad, I want to create an environment where my kids learn, grow and experience life to the full extent of their potential. And I will be ecstatic if they do it all to a higher level than I ever have or ever could. The fewer limits I place on their originality, uniqueness and special qualities, the more chance they have of doing just that. (Of course, that my kids being happy, healthy, wealthy and wise might encourage them to put dear old dad in an exclusive beach-front retirement flat in old age has nothing to with it).

Now apply this thinking to your business. If you don't give your employees the opportunity to lead, they will get frustrated and leave—most likely within a few weeks or months of being hired.

If you give them the opportunity to lead within strict guidelines and limits, they will also get frustrated and leave within a year or two.

If you give them the opportunity to lead to the full extent of their talent and potential, they can improve, enhance, grow and evolve your business better than any new machine, consultant, operating system or IT program even can.

Sure this can be dangerous. It can be a little risky. It can be very scary at times. Who cares? Everything in life that's worth having is worth taking a little risk to get your hands on. Little companies take little risks. Big companies take big risks. But little companies can also become big companies by taking big risks.

However, the price of leadership is responsibility: the greater the freedom to lead the greater the responsibility for that leadership.

This is actually Sir Isaac Newton's little known 4th Law from his management consulting days when he stopped playing around with apples and gravity and realised there was more money in performance consulting: there is a direct and linear relationship between leadership and responsibility.

And this is where the decentralised leadership model has fallen down. It sounds good; decentralised leadership, shared leadership, leadership teams, leadership groups, leader councils, empowerment circles, leadership through engagement— management models where organisations share the leadership load across several people providing them with the opportunity to contribute ideas, views and thoughts.

What we are seeing in society and particularly from the generations Y and I is a distinct 'my way' approach. It is the era of individualisation.

In the past, we have talked about teams in terms of 'we' not 'me'. Now we are looking at a prevailing attitude of 'me' *and* 'we'—the maximisation of the potential of each individual and the combining of individuals operating at their full potential into a functioning team.

Leadership without responsibility is like giving a teenager the keys to their first car without them having to learn to drive: things may seem to be going really fast at first but it is very dangerous.

A football team I was working with decided that they would appoint a players' representative group—a leadership team—to liaise between the players and the coaches/management on relevant issues. At first these issues were limited to social activities, the venue for the end-of-year holiday and the colour of their training wear. Over the season, the leadership group grew as leaders and became more confident in their leadership roles— which was exciting. They wanted more and more input into important areas like team tactics, team training and even team selections. For one reason, the coach was a little confronted by this. The players wanted to lead, to make decisions and to provide direction for the team in areas which could significantly influence the outcome of games, but they were not prepared to accept any of the responsibility for the outcomes of those decisions. In short; if the team won, it was the players who took responsibility, but if they lost... it was the coach's fault. It wasn't long before the coach went back to the old leadership by dictatorship model—with his favourite catchphrase: the best committee is a committee of one.

Managers who embrace the trendy 'engagement and empowerment' models of leadership need to ensure that the not so trendy 'responsibility and accountability' model runs parallel and complimentary to them.

It is critical that people are given the opportunity to learn to lead, to explore their potential and are given the freedom to demonstrate their unique talents and abilities. But it is just as critical they accept the responsibility and accountability for this freedom.

Story time...

I was talking with one the world's leading football coaches about leadership and his way of looking at things was refreshing. He said; "I believe the best leadership is no leadership."

Obviously, a comment like that needed a follow up question; "What do you mean?"

He replied; "In the old days there was no leadership. The head coach decided what everyone was going to do, when they were going to do it, and how they were going to do it—and that was it. It wasn't leadership, it was telling and yelling. Then we went through a phase when we started to appoint captains, then captains and vice captains. We started to embrace the concept of leadership and one of its core qualities—that leaders create other leaders. We started to hand over the responsibility for leadership to others.

"Then the leadership group concept got all trendy, and we saw sporting teams appoint several leaders within their team—each one responsible for a different aspect of team behaviour or attitude or logistics, etc.

"We're now at the stage where we don't want leaders in the traditional sense. We want each member of the team; players, coaches, and staff to willingly and unconditionally accept full responsibility and accountability for their own leadership. We want them to lead themselves and ensure everything they do is the best it can be. In effect, we don't need leaders, we need people who consistently do everything they do to the best of their ability. The impact of that—having everyone in the organisation leading themselves—will result in the development of an unstoppable team."

LESSONS IN NOT LEADING—WHAT DIDN'T YOU LEARN?

1. Leadership and responsibility—two sides of the same coin.

2. Creating the next generation of leaders can be risky but very rewarding.

3. Individuals working at their full potential—working together as a group working at full potential—can achieve anything.

Chapter Thirteen

Teams—why they don't really exist either

I have been fortunate to work with some outstanding sporting teams and winning sporting clubs all over the world. They are all unique, living, breathing things, but they all have three things in common:

1.Winning clubs have at their heart a winning culture, built on relevant and meaningful values like respect, honesty, selflessness, integrity and a commitment to something greater than themselves. They start with this at their core, then they build a winning team around their culture—a culture which grows from within—one that is owned by and driven by coaches, players and staff with real integrity, honesty, humility, passion, trust and commitment to a common goal.

2.Winning clubs create and grow a champion team—they do not buy a team of champions. It is next to impossible to buy a championship winning team—you have to grow one. Big egos, selfishness, mercenary attitudes and dishonesty have no place in a winning professional football team and ultimately bring the club unstuck.

3.Winning clubs have an egalitarian approach to team success. There are no 'rock stars'—no one person who is bigger than the rest of the team. Everyone works hard and contributes to the success of the team. Views, opinions, and unique talents of all individuals, from the head coach to the best player to the guy who cleans the boots and makes up the sports drinks, are all equally respected.

Many professional teams have attempted to buy a winning culture by recruiting the best players, coaches and staff, throwing them together and then sitting back to wait for the trophies to roll in. This rarely—if ever—works.

A Ferrari fitted with Ducati brakes, a Honda transmission, a Porsche engine, a Renault body and a Jaguar suspension system does not make a great racing car. The best cars in the world are built from the ground up with parts and components designed to fit together to produce maximum performance. Buying the best parts available, bolting them together and sending the car out to win an F1 is ludicrous.

In the past, you could build teams by artificially and superficially bringing them together under a banner or logo. Or you could bring people together, find some common ground and set some goals to achieve as a team.

You tried to create loyalty. Loyalty to an organisation. Loyalty to a jersey. Loyalty to a club. Loyalty to a flag or ideal. Loyalty to a nation.

The problem is loyalty is dead. The concept of loyalty as we knew it is dead. People change jobs and even careers many times in their working life. Professional athletes change clubs for more money and better opportunities. The divorce rate is over 50 percent in most western countries. People change city, state and even country for better opportunities for them and their families. Loyalty does not exist and is no longer an effective motivational tool.

The only loyalty that has any real meaning is self-loyalty—to be loyal to what's real, to people, relationships and experiences that have meaning and to things that have value to you. So you need to understand what you value most. Once you understand that, you can look for similar values and beliefs and passion in others and find a common starting point for building an effective team.

Throwing people together under a flag or banner or colour or company logo is not working any more. The team building icons and team development tools we have used in the past are no longer relevant. People will form effective, enthusiastic and excellent teams only when organisations show a real understanding and a genuine interest in the needs and values of each individual in that team.

A leading professional team I worked with had a creed: Passion, Honesty and Toughness. These words had become a doctrine, an institution, at the club and were passed down through generations of players for almost 75 years.

The words were written on the walls, on the entrance to the club, even on letterheads. Everyone—players, coaches, managers, board, fans, sponsors and media—all knew the Passion, Honesty and Toughness code. Some senior players even had the words tattooed on their bodies to demonstrate their pride and passion.

At our first session, I wrote those words up on the board and asked some younger players, players who has just joined the team in the off season, what the creed meant to them. The general response was, "nothing".

One of the senior players commented; "But this code has defined our club. It's what we've always been about. It says who we are and what we do." To this a young player replied; "That's great—but what does it mean to me?"

The important issue was what was important for this group? What had meaning, value and relevance for this year's team and this group of players? How could they make the code personal so they felt ownership of the code and could use it to enhance their own performances in the coming season?

This new direction in team development has presented a very real challenge to many organisations. The old team development model was an easy one to understand and implement. The board and management decided what the organisation was about, what the products and services would be, what the company logo and image would be and how the people they hired would deliver it all. They then got HR to put it all in a rule book—the despised HR manual—and people practiced the doctrine according to St Ford of Detroit, St McDonalds of Illinois or St Microsoft of Silicon Valley. Organisations created teams by ensuring the people in those teams thought, believed and acted the way the organisations wanted them to.

In reality, things are now reversed—team building is now upside down. Organisations can not define teams—teams (and the individuals who make up those teams)—define organisations. Boards and management need to accept their organisations must be more dynamic and fluid and prepared to change more frequently and radically than ever before.

The current Generation Y and future generations (has anyone figured out what we will call people once we get passed generation I?) do not and will not accept team development by company doctrine. If they don't own it and don't believe in it and it does not have direct, personal relevance or value to them, they will not form an effective team and help to grow the organisation.

In the old days, organisations trying to create teams worked from outside to inside, from big to little, from macro to micro. Companies determined what teams would deliver and, when, where and how they would deliver it.

Now, the successful companies build teams from inside to outside. They provide the environment and opportunity for teams to grow and develop and flourish by providing the environment and opportunity for individuals to grow, develop and flourish.

People create teams—teams do not create people.

Story time...

There's a big difference between knowledge and understanding.

A professional team I was working with wanted me to look at their overall organisational philosophies and values. The problem was, which ones did they want me to look at? First there were the overall organisational values, which had been in place for over 20 years: People, Passion and Performance. Then there were the team values, which had been pulled together by a group of players and coaches around five years ago: Commitment, Hard Work and Professionalism. And, the current player group, working with a management consultancy firm also developed their own values for this team and this season: Intensity, Dedication and Honesty. Plus... the coaching group had decided to base its coaching program around a simple creed, which would underpin the way they coached the team this year: Clarity, Execution and Relentlessness. And, finally... the player leadership group had come up with a set of values that would form the platform for their decision making and leadership of the team this season: Humility, Integrity and Courage.

It was like trying to sort a pile of newspapers in the middle of a hurricane. What was the solution?

We sat the entire organisation down together in two lines facing each other, each person sitting knees to knees across from one other person. The group was instructed to look at the person sitting in front of them and ask them "why are you here?" i.e. why have you decided to be here—to work in this organisation—at this moment in time?

The next instruction was; "No matter the answer the person opposite you gives… ask them again, "why are you here?" And if you feel it's necessary, ask them a third and even a fourth time until you feel that what they're telling you is an accurate and honest account of what's motivating them to be here at this moment in time.

Over the next hour we repeated this exercise several more times—each time changing partners—so that everyone had the opportunity to connect with at least 10 other people in the organisation and ask them about their motivation for working there.

I then asked the group; "What did you learn?"

One of the office staff members stood up and said; "I learnt that everyone is here for different reasons. John is here to earn enough money to pay off his house. Stephanie is here because she loves sport and wants to be in the industry. The Head Coach is here to do one thing… *win!* I had no idea people had so many reasons for being here."

I replied; "Great answer. But if that's the case, how do we build something special here that everyone can enjoy being a part of, where we can all achieve our individual and collective goals?"

One of the senior players suggested, "We need something simple, something easy to remember, something that will have meaning and relevance to everyone in the organisation regardless of who they are, what they do, or why they are here."

"Again, outstanding thinking," I said; "But what could that be?"

I suggested; "We know that the best people, the best organisations, are learning organisations. They have a thirst for learning, improvement and getting better at what they do. What about this? Instead of building your success on values—knowing there are so many values systems in this place—why not base it on learning? Why not, when you meet each other, see each other, greet each other, start every conversation, every email, every phone call with "what did you learn today?"

Everyone talks about change, yet change terrifies so many people. And people talk about values, but values mean different things to different people and even this changes at different times in their lives. But learning is the one thing common to all of us. We learn, we grow, we improve, we change, we get better and we'll all achieve what we're here to achieve.

LESSONS IN NOT LEADING—WHAT DIDN'T YOU LEARN?

1. Teams can be a powerful force in helping organisations to forge a successful future.

2. However, teams must be allowed to create and use their own energy—to give life and strength to the organisation.

3. The old team development models simply do not work in this century—it's *me* and then *we*.

Chapter Fourteen

Leadership opportunities and how to spot them

Leadership is like knowing the funniest joke in the world. It's great to know, it but what you really want is a chance to use it!

It's like having a new Ferrari. It's no good keeping it the garage. What you really want is to drive it down the main street so someone you know can see you behind the wheel.

In the bad old days of leadership training, we would try to bludgeon people to death with leadership seminars, leadership workshops, leadership programs, leadership training and so on and so forth. It was like those times when you were a kid and your Mum and Dad bought a bottle of some foul-tasting and awful-smelling tonic. You didn't want it and you sure as heck didn't enjoy it, but mum and dad justified it by saying stuff like; "this will do you good".

Also in the bad old days of leadership, we held meetings… long, dull, boring, tedious, drab, unexciting, mundane, energy-draining meetings. It's what leaders did.

Want to communicate with your team? Hold a meeting.

Want to inspire and motivate your team? Hold a meeting.

Want to generate new ideas and get people to contribute 'outside the box' thinking? Hold a meeting.

Meetings are without doubt the single greatest cause of failing leaders and leadership in the world. Some leaders are spending more time and energy preparing for and sitting in meetings than they spend doing actual work. Getting a bunch of people in a room and forcing them to share, to learn, to grow and to collaborate at that moment, in that situation is a recipe for disaster, and, above all, meetings are mostly a complete waste of time.

Why do people hold meetings? To communicate news and information? No. That's what phones, email and social media are for. To inspire and motivate? No. Inspiration needs to be done

one-on-one, in person and in an environment of respect, trust and understanding. And for the most part, motivating other people is a myth. To get people to share new and innovative 'outside the box' ideas? (The term 'outside the box' usually means "we need ideas which are just a little different to what we're currently doing—not too different—but just a fraction different so it looks like we're different even though we're not.") No. Very few people are capable of developing genuinely new, original and lateral creative ideas in a group setting—outside of some very talented individuals in places like Disney, DreamWorks and similar creative agencies.

The purpose of a meeting is to get people to act, to change, to do something, or to stop doing something. Meetings are about creating and stimulating action. And the best way to stimulate action is through connecting with other people in a way in which they want to connect.

Getting good at leadership means being good at identifying moments and opportunities when people are ready to be influenced, educated, inspired and led.

How do you spot the opportunity to lead?

1.When you hear any of the following words:
- Never
- Always
- Must
- Every
- Only

The best time to step up and lead is when someone else isn't. Sounds simple. And it is.

Words like 'never' and 'every' imply that the way things are, is the way things are and the ways things are will always be the way things are. This is a leader's greatest opportunity to lead.

The greatest opportunity for a leader to lead and the best environment to lead, is one where people have resigned themselves to routine, ritual and rational thinking, where people have placed rules, limits, restrictions and policies over the way they think and act.

Just remember: people who speak in absolutes are never right.

2.Anywhere people, organisations or industries are all doing the same thing.

Another great leadership opportunity is when people have all bought into doing the same thing, to follow a trend or an idea or a doctrine or a policy that everyone else is following. This is happening more with the expansion of the internet and easy access to the latest ideas, innovations and information. It's easier to search, copy, cut and paste than to innovate, think and create.

The most wonderful thing about an industry in which people and organisations are all doing the same as each other is the opportunity for talented people and lateral thinking leaders to make an impact. History is full of stories about people who resisted the urge to follow the crowd and dared to be different, who did the impossible and refused to allow the status quo to slow them down, and who rejected the limits and boundaries of the custodians of the contemporary 'truth'.

Leaders are different. They talk, act and behave differently. And, they are not afraid to show their difference when everyone else is telling them their difference is wrong, weird, strange or just plain stupid.

Mozart's music was considered too complex and his operas too long for people to enjoy. Picasso was told that his radical approach to art was infantile and no one would ever want to look at it or buy it. When Steve Jobs first started talking about his belief that computers the size of pocket calculators would one day connect everyone on earth he was considered a bit of a looney or maybe experiencing the after effects of a few years of substance abuse in college. Michael Phelps, the greatest ever Olympic athlete, whose individual medal winning achievements rival those of entire countries, would swim an extra 10,000 metres on his own early on Sunday mornings as part of his personal commitment to gain a winning edge over his opposition.

Difference wins!

3.Anywhere people think things are hopeless, hard, horrible and hideous.

Emotions bring out the best and worst in people. People show who they really are when they are very happy or when they are very sad. And this provides leaders with the best leadership opportunity. If you know and understand who someone is, you can help them. If you care about them, really, genuinely care about them as human beings, you'll recognise the times, the situations and the opportunities when leading them—the way they need to be led, or *not* led—can make all the difference to their lives.

I was working with a new professional football team—a new franchise. The beauty of working with a new franchise is that it's a clean slate. There's no history or bad habits or rituals or traditions to hold the players and coaches back from achieving success.

I was discussing the process of building a new team, a new culture, with the head coach, a very experienced coach who'd led other teams to success.

I asked; "What's the first step in building and growing a winning team?"

The coach responded; "See that big hill out there?"

"Yes," I said.

"That's the first step. Be here at 6am tomorrow morning."

The next morning, I arrived to see all the players standing at the bottom of the big hill. The coach addressed the group; "Morning guys. Get yourselves warmed up. Do some stretching and get ready for some running."

The coach then spoke to me; "I want you to watch and tell me what you see."

"Ok guys. I want you to run up and down that big hill over there as many times as you can in 30 minutes," said the coach. "I want you to give it all you've got. Leave nothing in the tank. Give it your absolute best."

And I watched. And this is what I saw. Some players immediately complained, moaned, whined and somehow, out of nowhere, found little injuries and strains that didn't appear to have been there before they were asked to run the big hill. A few players slumped and slouched their way to the base of the hill and begrudgingly started on their training exercise. Several other players jogged over to the hill and started running—appearing to be doing it more out compliance and the fear of the consequences of not doing it.

In the group, however, two players stood out. Not only did they run as fast as they could over to the big hill to commence their training but once they got there, they gave it all they had.

Over the next 30 minutes I saw every possible variation in running and training behaviour it is possible to see. Most players did what they were asked to do and ran more-or-less non-stop for 30 minutes. However, it was the way they did it that was interesting. Some ran fast for a little while—then relaxed and ran easily as they tired. Some players seemed to only work hard when the coaching staff were watching. A few others appeared to never extend themselves much at all. Those two players—the ones who had raced over to start the hill session were different. They pushed themselves, not just up the hill, but raced back down again. They gave all they had to every repetition. At ten minutes they seemed to be exhausted. But they kept going. At twenty minutes— covered in sweat, breathing heavily and incredibly fatigued—they kept going. With a few minutes to go, not only were they still giving all they had to the task, but they were encouraging other players to keep trying, even to the point of pushing and pulling a few team mates up the hill. It was inspirational.

After the session, I met with the coach and shared my observations.

He said; "I am a big believer in the saying 'the way you do anything, is the way do you everything'. Once we really know who these players are—without the pretence, without the games, without the bullshit—once we know who they are as people, we can start developing exceptional people and build a great team."

He went on; "That big hill is the same concept, the same philosophy as the boot camp-type training the military and the police use during recruit training. For us to build a strong, successful team, we need to see how the players respond to fatigue, to pressure, to personal challenge—the same situation and the same environment they'll face on the football field this year. Once we see who they are—once who they are is exposed honestly and without disguise, we can develop coaching strategies to help, support and develop them because we'll understand what it is they need to be the best they can be."

4.   Anywhere people are open, honest and willing to share their dreams.

Leadership opportunities present themselves to leaders, to friends, to family, to managers, to salespeople, to anyone who'd like to lead—when people look for them.

One of the greatest challenges, yet most magnificent opportunities for leaders is finding ways to lead people when they are looking for some kind of leadership. Many people are reluctant to open themselves up to leadership opportunities or to seek leadership of some kind unless:

· It's too late or almost too late—i.e. they are desperate
· The motivation to change and the potential reward of changing is much greater than the pain and consequences of NOT changing
· They've hit a point in their life where they realise they need help to realise their potential, i.e. the "I am running out of time" moment
· All the above

Regardless of why they are seeking leadership, once someone opens their heart and mind to learning and leadership, the leader must recognise the opportunity to lead needs to be focused on the TRUST principle.

· T (Team) Leadership is a team activity
· R (Responsibility) It is a shared responsibility
· U (Unity) Leader and learner working together
· S (Selfless) Leadership through putting the needs and the dreams of the learner first
· T (Time) Identify the moment and the opportunity to provide appropriate, relevant and meaningful leadership

Trust in any situation, in any environment, is powerful. Once people have developed an authentic, genuine personal connection based on trust, honesty starts to grow.

Honesty is a prized and difficult value to build in any organisation, but like trust, it is a powerful force for change, for success, for learning and for leadership.

Why are trust and honesty so powerful, so important, in successful organisations? Because if the relationships in the organisation are based on trust and honesty, people can communicate directly, sincerely, and effectively and that means people, and the organisation, can and will get better at what they do sooner.

There's no need to sugar-coat feedback because in an organisation built on trust and honesty, feedback is valued, it is prized, it is welcomed and it is actively sought as a cornerstone of personal and professional improvement.

In trusting, honest organisations, it's unnecessary to water-down suggestions for improvement or to sweeten ways of helping people to enhance their performance because everyone in the team knows advice, support, guidance and leadership are all given selflessly without political agendas or personal manipulations. In other words, where there's trust and honesty, people learn faster, grow quicker and improve sooner—everyone wins!

Story time...

A great friend of mine had coached an Olympic gold medallist. We were talking one day about coaching, about leadership, about winning, about success, about all the things he'd learnt working with his athlete on their Olympic journey.

He said; "It's all about identifying the opportunities to make a difference. There are times when an athlete is looking for coaching. There are times when an athlete wants to be left alone and work things out, to solve problems themselves. The art of coaching is very much about identifying the opportunities to coach and when not to."

He continued, "I often think when the difference between winning and losing at the Olympics comes down to fractions of a second, how many of those fractions were due to coaches missing opportunities to coach? For whatever reason, they couldn't or didn't see those moments when their coaching and their leadership could have made a difference. And even more important, I wonder what are the cumulative effects of those missed coaching and leadership opportunities over the life of an athlete?

LESSONS IN NOT LEADING — WHAT DIDN'T YOU LEARN?

1. There are opportunities to lead everywhere. You just need to learn how to spot them.
2. The best leadership opportunities come out of situations where people are all doing the same thing. Great leadership, modern leadership, is all about uniqueness and being different.
3. There's no better opportunity to lead than when no one else is.

Chapter Fifteen

Developing Leaders and Leadership—the only training course you'll ever need

Life doesn't come with an instruction book. There isn't a course or program or manual which says; "Julie Wilson: how to maximise my potential, find happiness and true contentment over the next 83 years." No one is gifted at birth with a white folder marked with large letters, 'Tony Johnson: Your guide to the next 75 years'.

And even if it did exist, no one would probably read their own manual, or they would skip the first few pages and look for the juicy bits, or maybe even turn to the back and find out when it all ends.

Some people spend a lot of their lives looking for their instruction manual. Most try the formal education system. Some try religion. A few worship moon rocks and Christmas beetles and find their life manual written on the underside of banana leaves. And way too many do leadership training courses and self-help programs and believe they can buy the secret to long life, health, wealth and happiness.

So, to keep you happy here it is. The *Leading Without Leading* training course—your own personal instruction manual.

Learning to Lead Without Leading—Step One: Sit down with someone you know and trust and ask them to tell you with complete, total, uncompromising, brutal, punch-in-the-nose, kick-in-the guts, no-holds-barred, boots-and-all honesty—about you. For some of us, this could be a friend or family member. For others, it could be a professional like a psychologist, life coach or doctor. But choose someone who can tell it to you straight.

This first step is so critical, so important, so vital—but potentially so painful and difficult that most people avoid it. Real honesty is a rare commodity, and like rare commodities, it is special, hard to find, valuable and worth seeking.

Most people avoid total honesty because it's tough. Real honesty is like an exercise program. We all know it is good for us and can help us achieve great things in life, but sometimes it hurts like hell, so we avoid it as much as possible.

Everyone plays roles. In the morning, you are Dad or Mum. On the way to work you are a commuter. At work you are the boss, the employee, the analyst, the manager or the engineer. At lunch time, you are the jogger or corporate meeting-er. In the evening, you are student or cook or shopper or just hanging out relaxing at home-er. But who are you really?

Most people play these different roles because of the time, place or situation they are in at the time. Go to the park with the kids— you are Dad. Present some ideas at a meeting—you are marketing manager. Go out to dinner with your partner—you are husband or wife. We all play different roles at different times. But who are you really?

Learning to lead yourself means figuring out who yourself is... yourself. And this requires real honesty. As most people lack the courage, knowledge, capacity and will to be 100 percent honest about themselves, ask someone who can. It will be the greatest investment in your life, your loves, and your leadership you will ever make.

Learning to Lead Without Leading—Step Two: Decide what's important, what you value, what has meaning for you. Whether you are leading yourself or leading others, it is vital you know and understand who you are and what you value.

A corporate client I was working with asked me to help figure out what he wanted out of life. I didn't know him well, so I asked him to bring in a box of his favourite photos—the ones he valued the most. We spent about an hour looking through photos of his Mum and his Dad, his brother and sisters, his childhood pets, his school friends, the house he grew up in, the holiday house his family leased every summer, all the people, places and things he valued as a young boy. Of all the photos in the box, one seemed to touch him more than any other. It was a photo of him playing with a small truck when he was about ten years old. He said, "I used to dream about building things. I was always at my happiest building and creating stuff. I had forgotten that. I had forgotten what I really value. I had forgotten what's really important to me."

Do the photo exercise yourself. Dig out some old photos, you know those old, funny-looking and funny-smelling ones in that old shoe box you have kept with you for 20 years but haven't looked at since the moon landing (assuming there actually *was* a moon landing). Spend time looking at you. What did you love doing? Who were you favourite friends? What things did you enjoy thinking about and doing? When you thought what thoughts did you think? What made you happy? What scared you? What excited you (apart from lollies, super heroes, Barbie and watching afternoon TV)?

Psychologists tell us that who we are, what we valued and what we believed by about age ten is pretty much who we will be, what we will value and what we will believe for the rest of your life. Sure, some things will change; your hairstyle, your taste in clothes. Your priorities will shift from M&Ms to rum and coke, from Barbies to beach wear, from frogs to furniture, and from biscuits to beer, but the things that make you you—the core things that have real meaning—are pretty much there before you hit high school.

You need to understand who you really are in order to lead who you really are and to realise your potential as a leader and a human being.

Learning to Lead Without Leading—Step Three: Lead yourself! Then inspire others to do the same.

Once you know who you are, what you value and you have honestly, sincerely and genuinely figured out what you are about, you can lead with confidence, calmness, composure, compassion and creativity.

The other way—the "I don't know who I am, what I want, what I value, where I am going or where I want to end up," does not and cannot work.

The beauty about this new leadership is in *not* leading. You don't have to tell anyone what to do. You don't have to instruct. You don't have to indoctrinate. You don't have to intimidate. You don't have to inculcate.

All you need to do is illuminate, inspire and encourage. Provide the environment and opportunity for people to learn to lead and they will do it themselves. Once the people around you see the benefits of being themselves and leading by being true to who they are, they will join the team, climb on board, step up to the mark, raise the bar, click into gear and any of the thousand other leadership clichés you can think of.

The new leadership is not telling people they should do things your way, it's inspiring others to follow their own dreams and lead their way.

Learning to Lead Without Leadership—Step Four: Be yourself: Back yourself.

Believe. Believe. Believe.

As you explore your own leadership and express your uniqueness as a leader, you will catch YEAHBUTWHATIF disease, which, if left untreated, is fatal. In terms of your leadership, if YEAHBUTWHATIF takes hold, you are dead.

"Yeahbutwhatif I am not good enough?"

"Yeahbutwhatif people don't like me or my ideas?"

"Yeahbutwhatif people don't like what I am doing because I am doing it differently?"

Believe. Believe. Believe.

Some people will think you are not good enough. I am sure of it. Some people will not like you and will hate your ideas. You can guarantee it. Some people will think you have lost your mind. Almost certainly. But remember... at every stage in history people who thought, dreamed and acted differently—people like you—came up with ideas and innovations that changed the world.

People knew the world was flat until someone came along and thought differently. People knew the earth was the centre of the universe before someone came along and thought differently.

People knew it was impossible to fly to the moon until someone thought differently and proved it was (or was it?).

To those who think differently and believe in their uniqueness, anything is possible.

Story time…

Off all the values sporting teams aspire to and believe essential to their success, honesty is the number one.

I can't count the times I've been working with a professional team or a sporting organisation, designed and delivered a training session about values and had the group decide that honesty was the one core value they wanted to underpin their team culture.

And in all of those times and situations where honesty has been identified as *the* most important value in the organisation, I've asked them the same question… what does honesty look like?

The best answer to that question I've heard so far has been this one; "honesty is being true to who you are."

The person I first heard that phrase from told me a story. "Once," she said, "I was talking with my grandfather. He was in his mid 70s and I was in my early 20s. I asked him about his life and if he had his time over again what—if anything—would he do differently?

"He sighed and said; 'I'd be myself more often.'

"I asked him what he meant by that.

"He replied, 'It's taken me 70-odd years to figure out I was pretty much born with all I needed to know somewhere in my head. I travelled a lot. I had some amazing experiences. Saw some incredible things. But I know now that the times I felt happiest—the times when I was at peace, the times when I felt that everything in life was the way it needed to be—was when I was just being me. When I actually did things I knew instinctively were right—things that were inside my heart, things that were somehow always there—everything seemed to flow nicely for me. It's taken me over 70 years to understand that all I needed to do to be happy was to be myself more often instead of trying to be someone I wished I could be or go somewhere I'd always wanted to go. If I'd have been me more often life would have been a whole lot easier, kinder and sweeter.'"

LESSONS IN NOT LEADING—WHAT DIDN'T YOU LEARN?

1. Be yourself.

2. Believe in yourself.

3. Back yourself.

Chapter Sixteen

So… what did you learn about not leading?

My Dad's name was Bill.

Bill was a smart guy. Not academic smart, but like a lot of dads of his era (he was born in 1923), smart all the same. He had lived through some tough times, survived a few years serving overseas in World War II, battled through the Depression and learnt a lot of life lessons the hard way.

He told me this story many, many times (one sure sign you have become a dad is to tell the same stories and jokes over and over and forget you have told them).

This was a Bill special: When you're five years old, you know nothing. Everything is new and interesting. You learn new stuff every day. It's a wonderful and exciting time of your life, because learning is life.

When you're 15 years old, you know everything. Mum, Dad, teachers, neighbours, coaches, they are all dummies. You know it all, you've seen it all, done it all. No one can tell you anything. You don't listen to anyone except your friends—who are as busy not listening to or learning from anyone else. And you don't learn much at all.

When you're 25 years old, and have been in the workforce for a few years, you start to realise there might be a few things you don't know—but you are usually having too good a time to bother taking the time to learn them.

When you're 35 years old, you start thinking there's a lot of stuff you don't know. And you might embark on a course or a program, or start reading self-help books and trying to kick-start the old brain again.

When you're 45 years old, you realise all of a sudden that you know nothing and that's when you start learning like a 5-year-old all over again. And your life becomes all the better for it.

And that's where I hope you are now. Like the 45-year-old, accepting that in terms of leadership, you know nothing. Because that's when you will learn to lead more effectively than ever before.

At five we were invincible. At five super heroes were real. At five mum and dad knew everything and could make anything happen. At five there was still a chance you might learn to fly. And at five follow the leader had no rules, no limits, no boundaries, no restrictions. Leading was just being you and doing what you wanted to do.

When it comes to leadership, we *know* nothing. That is because there are no rules, no limits, no boundaries, no barriers, no guidelines and no restrictions. We can't in all honesty say we have found the definitive answer to how to become a great leader.

So, what do we know?

We know that everyone has the potential to lead. We know that everyone has to lead their own way. We know that leadership means change, innovation, uniqueness and individuality. We know that many people find the concept of being different and unique and unusual challenging and the notion of conformity much more comforting than conflict.

But to be able to say; "And this is exactly what leadership is..."—no one knows. Lots of people claim to know. Everyone has a theory, or concept, or equation, or principle, or checklist, but no one knows for sure.

The only thing I know about leadership for sure is that anyone who stands up and claims they've got the answer, that they've developed the one true leadership program, the best, all singing, all dancing, all knowing leadership training system, is the *one* person I wouldn't be listening to.

It's a leadership 'land-rush': no one owns the best way to develop leaders or leadership. The academics haven't got it right. The management consultancies haven't either. Neither have the politicians or philosophers. And that's the most fantastic thing about it!

These are exciting times for leadership. There is a leadership revolution going on because the whole idea of leadership has been redefined. And it hasn't been the current crop of leaders who have redefined it. Leadership is now being driven by a new generation who learn faster, think quicker, make better decisions, want more, want it now, want it to be enjoyable, and want it to be something uniquely theirs. How fantastic is that?

Not only that, but if you are a leader now—a CEO or director or board member or manager or supervisor or foreman—you now have permission to get out and lead better than ever before. You have a mandate for change, for accelerating the rate of change at an unheard of speed and to explore your own leadership potential to beyond anything you ever thought possible.

Why? Because the people you are hiring now, and will hire in the future, will demand it. They want to be a part of something that is growing, learning, changing, and improving with dynamic energy, and they want to work with leaders as passionate about change and exploring new possibilities as they are.

More than ever your own leadership potential and your uniqueness can be the way for you to realise your dreams.

The government will not save us from global warming, the next big financial crisis or solve world hunger (don't forget it was largely their attitudes, their policies and their lack of leadership that got us into this mess). Nor will new legislation, new corporate rules or a re-hashed bunch of international financial market regulations. Neither will a leadership guru. Or a course. Or a workshop. Or a program.

No one is going to come and turn it all around and make it so that the flowers bloom brighter, the sun shines shinier and the air smells cleaner. The only person who can—and will—change it for you, is you.

The challenge for all of us is to think globally but act locally. That is—be aware of what's happening around the world but control the controllables, act to be the best you can be each day. Control your own reactions to what's happening, manage your own behaviour, drive your own attitudes and change what you need to change in your own life and in your own workplace.

Don't wait for the world to turn around and then filter down to you. Change your own world and inspire change in the people and places around you.

Set high standards in all you do. Be the industry standard. Set the industry lead. Someone has to—why not you? Why can't you be the best in the world? Why can't you be the best in Australia? Or Singapore? Or New Zealand? Or the US? You can.

Inspire behaviour change—you can't enforce it or make it happen—change comes from the inside.

Let's inspire people to change, to become more aware and to commit to the need for change in their daily behaviours. This is not about selling, it's about leadership, about your own leadership and about encouraging the development of leadership in others.

Some people seem to feel the need to ask someone else to give them permission to lead—that is for someone to help provide inspiration for them to be leaders, to be the industry standard and to set new levels of excellence in what is ostensibly difficult financial times.

Turn this around. Challenge each person to be the best they can be in all things every day and to take up the challenge to become *the* industry leader in what they do.

Rapidly changing times means there is an opportunity for someone in the insurance industry and the car industry and health care industry and manufacturing industry and every industry, to become the world leader in the business as it moves forward—why can't it be you and the people you work with?

Freddie Einstein—Albert's little known and little respected little brother—took scientific theories and real estate to another level when he said; "Forget matter. Money and Opportunity are neither created nor destroyed—they are just passed around between people."

He was right. There is as much money and opportunity around now as there ever was—it's just that the location of that money and those opportunities has shifted.

So what are you waiting for? Go find them!

The first step in any journey is critical. Before you get to the end of this book, stop. Stop and make a commitment to a single change and to taking the first step in what is the rest of your life. But do it and do it now and commit to making it happen.

Story time...

I travelled away to work with a local government organisation. I was there to conduct a two-day workshop on sport and how to grow sporting clubs. On the afternoon I arrived I had a few hours to rest and recover from the travel so I went for a walk along the bike trail running outside my hotel.

After about 15 minutes, I saw a skate park. There was one kid, around 13 years of age, in the park practicing. He was just a kid riding his board on a sunny afternoon. I saw him try to ride his board up the side of a concrete bank... and he fell off.

As a father of four kids, my first impulse was to rush in and help him, but he didn't need my help... he got up, adjusted his helmet, checked out his board and went back to where he'd started.

He then took off and raced up the concrete bank, and again he fell.

I stood there watching him as he tried again and again to defeat his concrete foe.

Eight times. Nine times. Ten times... over and over he'd push off on his board, race up to the obstacle, try his best to overcome the challenge and fall.

I couldn't help myself. I went over and asked; "Are you ok?

He looked at me a bit suspiciously and replied; "Sure. I'm cool".

I said, "I'm a coach. I wish I could get my athletes to train as hard as you do. I wish I could get them to sacrifice as much time as you do getting better and to work as hard as you are working."

He looked at me like I was an idiot.

"You can't be much of a coach if you have to push your athletes to do stuff... maybe they just don't like training. I'm not sacrificing anything, this is what I love to do. Me and my friends have been trying to beat this damn (concrete) bank for the past month and no one's got close yet. So, I decided to come down every day after school and keep at it until I can do it."

Lessons in leadership are everywhere!

Passion drives performance.

Commitment determines outcome.

Leadership is nothing more than having a dream to chase and never relenting until that dream becomes a reality. Whether it's motivating yourself to chase the dream or inspiring others to chase theirs, leadership begins and ends with a personal decision to change and to make a difference.

Prologue

Interesting stuff to look at and read

Books:

•*Daring Greatly: How the Courage to Be Vulnerable Transforms the Way We Live, Love, Parent, and Lead* by Brené Brown

•*First, Break All the Rules: What the World's Greatest Managers Do Differently* by Marcus Buckingham and Curt Coffman

•*Man's Search for Meaning:* Viktor E. Frankl

•*Leading: Learning from Life and My Years at Manchester United* by Sir Alex Ferguson and Michael Moritz.

•*Tribes: We Need You to Lead Us* by Seth Godin

•*Eleven Rings: The Soul of Success* by Phil Jackson.

•*The Truth about Leadership: The No-Fads, Heart-Of-The-Matter Facts You Need to Know* by James M. Kouzes and Barry Z. Posner

•*The Five Dysfunctions of a Team:* A Leadership Fable by Patrick Lencioni

•*Drive* by Daniel H Pink

•*Lean In: Women, Work, and the Will to Lead* by Sheryl Sandberg and Nell Scovell

•*Start With Why* by Simon Sinek

• *Extreme Ownership: How U.S. Navy SEALs Lead and Win* by Jocko Willink and Leif Babin

Websites:
Dilbert http://dilbert.com/
The Harvard Business Review https://hbr.org/
The R.S.A. https://www.thersa.org/
TED https://www.ted.com/

About the Author

Wayne Goldsmith has worked in sport—at all levels—and all over the world for the past 25 years. Throughout that time, and over a remarkably varied and successful career, he's developed an understanding of leaders and leadership that's unique in its scope and practicality.

He's toured Europe with the Wallabies rugby team, walked on deck with the swimmers and coaches of the USA swimming team, warmed up with the Australian cricket team before a match, been on the field, in the change-rooms and in the coaching box on National Rugby League Grand Final Day as part of a professional football team, led an Olympic team at an Olympic Games and been invited to tell the New Zealand Rugby Union's High Performance Unit how it can get better at getting better.

As an industry leader, an educator, a coach, a consultant, a teacher, a writer, and a father of four, his first-hand experience of leadership in sport is unparalleled.

Where most sports professionals can share their ideas on success from one sport or one performance, Wayne's broad experience across so many Olympic and professional sports in over 30 nations gives him rare insights into the common factors that lead the best people in the world to victory.

His clients have included some of sport's leading performers:
- AFL teams (including the Brisbane Lions, North Melbourne Kangaroos and Port Adelaide Football Club)
- NRL teams (including the Wests-Tigers, Sydney Roosters and Gold Coast Titans)
- Super Rugby teams (including the ACT Brumbies, Queensland Reds, Canterbury Crusaders and the Western Force)
- Tennis Australia and the Australian Open Grand Slam tournament
- Professional netball (including Netball QLD / Firebirds and Netball NSW / Sydney Swifts)
- National sporting organisations including Swimming Australia, Triathlon Australia, Diving Australia, the Australian Rugby Union and the New Zealand Rugby Union
- Racing Victoria—responsible for Australia's most prestigious horse race, the Melbourne Cup
- Harness Racing NSW
- Kart-Sport NZ
- National and state government sporting bodies including the Australian Sports Commission, the Australian Institute of Sport, Sport New Zealand, the Singapore Sports Council, the Philippines

Olympic Committee and the QLD Department of National Parks, Sport and Racing

- More than 100 other regional and local sporting clubs, organisations and governments

Accolades

Wayne's coaching, thinking, writing and teaching have influenced some of the world's leading athletes, coaches and teams. He has been Chairman of several high-profile and innovative performance committees including:

- The Swimming Australia Sports Science and Sports Medicine and Research Committee
- The Triathlon Australia Sports Science, Sports Medicine and Research Committee
- The Australian Rugby Union Sports Science, Sports Medicine, Innovations and Research Committee
- The Brumbies Rugby Union Innovations Group

He is a winner of the Eunice Gill Prize for Outstanding Contribution to Coach Education in Australia and the Outstanding Contribution to Swimming in Australia Award. He also won the Mohammed Bin Rashid Al Maktoum Creative Sports Award.

In addition, Wayne is regularly invited to speak and present at corporate events and business functions across the real estate, banking, finance, investment, manufacturing, building, human resource, medical and education sectors.

Wayne lives in Australia on the Gold Coast with his wife and four children.

To contact Wayne, or to read and watch more of his work:
Wayne Goldsmith
Phone: +61 414 712 074
Email: wayne@moregold.com.au
Skype: waynemoregoldsmith
Website: http://wgcoaching.com/
Website: http://newsportfuture.com/
Facebook: https://www.facebook.com/TheCoachingBrain
Twitter: https://twitter.com/CoachingBrain
YouTube: https://www.youtube.com/wgcoaching

Made in the USA
Middletown, DE
27 July 2018